Civil War Letters and Diary of Joshua Winters

Civil War Letters and Diary of Joshua Winters

A Private in the Union Army
Company G, First Western Virginia
Volunteer Infantry

Editing and Introduction by
Elizabeth Davis Swiger
Fairmont, West Virginia

McClain Printing Company
Parsons, West Virginia
1991

International Standard Book Number 0-9616245-3-1
Library of Congress Catalog Card Number 91-90851
Printed in the United States of America

Second Printing 1996

Cover Design by Robert L. Heffner, Jr.

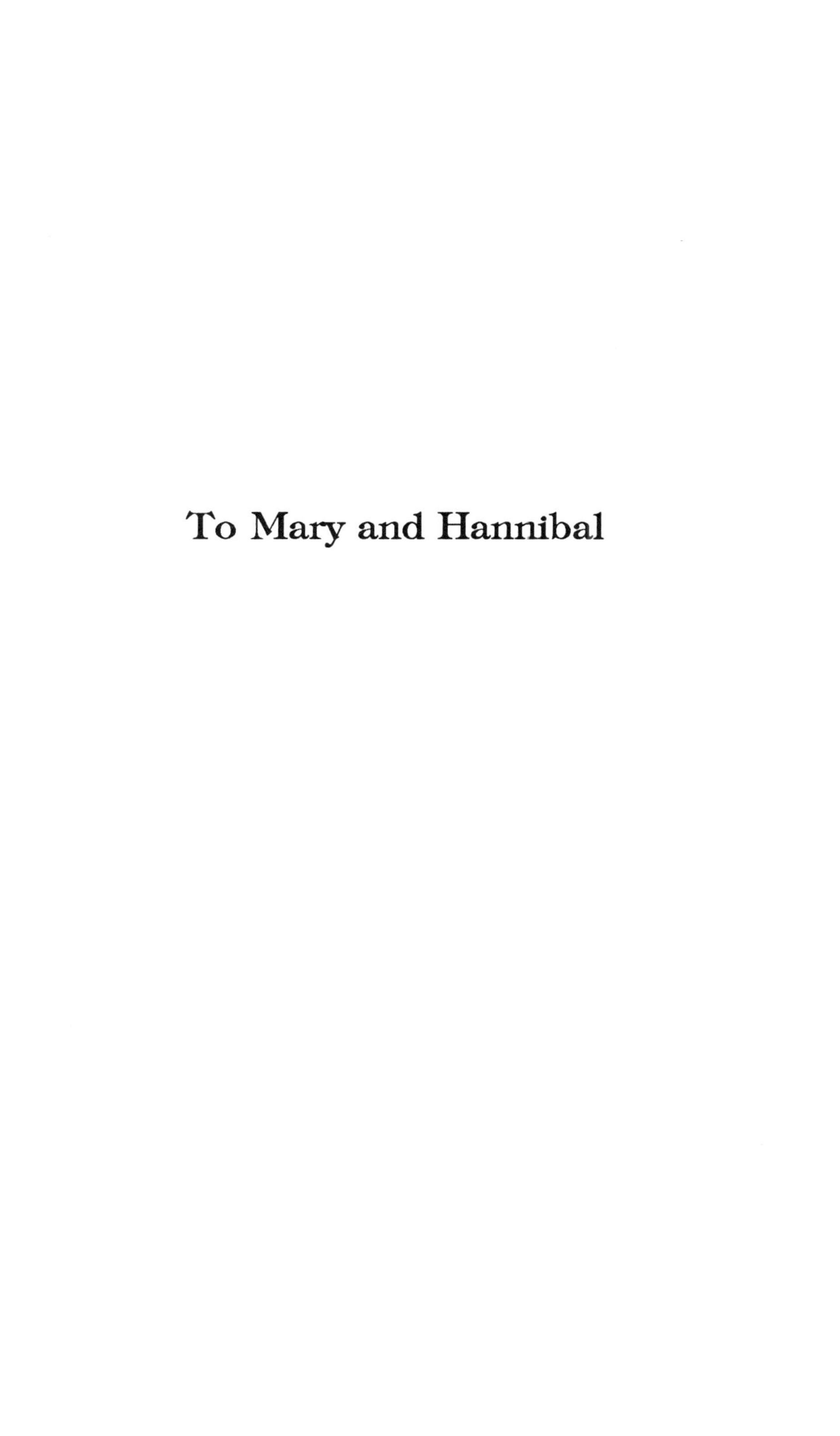

To Mary and Hannibal

Contents

Joshua Winters
1843 - 1900

Civil War Letters and Diary of Joshua Winters

Introduction

Joshua Winters and His World

Joshua Winters, the youngest son of John and Eliza (Davis) Winters, was born in what is now Sand Hill District, Marshall County, West Virginia, on 8 January 1843. He attended a school in Sand Hill located not far from his home. Textbooks survive inscribed by his brother, Isaac, and later by his younger sisters who had used them in turn, covering the subjects of Geography and Spelling. It is uncertain whether or not he attended school for the entire eight years.

The village of Sand Hill consisted of a Methodist church, a cemetery, a store (operated by the Marsh family), a blacksmith shop and a few clustered houses. The church is still active and still attended by some of Joshua's brother's descendants.[1] The village is no longer in existence. Area residents lived on farms, usually of 100-300 acres, so that "neighbors" may have lived several miles away. Nearly everyone in the district was considered a neighbor. A larger village, now known as Dallas WV, was called Haneytown in Civil War times. It was about four miles from the Winters home, to the east. Only a little further to the northwest was the edge of Wheeling, known as Elm Grove and commonly called "The Grove," with the "big city" of Wheeling just beyond. The county seat of Marshall County, Moundsville, was much further away and harder to get to. No one went there unless one needed to go to the courthouse to record a birth or death or a land transaction. Because of the

---

[1] Joshua's great-niece, Alta (Winters) McNinch, lives on an historic family farm and plays the piano for Sunday school and church at Sand Hill United Methodist Church every Sunday. (She died in 1995.)

difficulty in getting to Moundsville, many of the Sand Hill Civil War era births and deaths were not recorded until much later, or not at all. Remember that transportation was by walking, horseback, or horse-drawn buggy. Joshua did a lot of walking, not only as a youth but also as a soldier

Joshua, like nearly every other kid in Sand Hill District, lived on a farm. His father, John, owned several hundred acres in the area, some acquired from his father, Daniel, and many parcels purchased by himself.[2] On the farm, a boy learned to work hard and to organize his work for efficiency. Most farm labor was done by hand. Flax was grown, scutched, and eventually spun into thread and woven into cloth. Wool came from shearing sheep, carding, spinning and weaving. Nearly all the girls' clothes were homemade, but some yardgoods, especially cotton, were purchased. Quilts and blankets were homemade, warm and beautiful. Fruit and vegetables were grown on the farm, used in the summer and preserved for winter use. Wheat and corn were taken to a nearby mill and ground into flour and "meal". None of the Winters families had their own mill so far as we know. Everyone had hogs, chickens, milk cows and work horses and all the animal food was grown on the farm. Wood was chopped and stacked for use as fuel for cooking and for heating. Soap was made from wood ashes and lard or other fat. Candles were made by pouring molten tallow into candle molds, using flax wicks. Food was generally plentiful but cash was scarce. Cash came from taking excess produce to Wheeling to the Farmers' Market, or arranging with other farmers to sell or trade. Calves, pigs, and horses could also be sold. Coffee, tea, and sugar were purchased.

The Winters family never owned slaves. In fact, few slaves ever lived in the region, especially as late as the 1850's. The farm work was done by the parents and children. Sometimes there were extra people living with various families. These could have been cousins whose mother had died in childbirth, or other unattached young people. They worked basically for their room and board and so helped out on the farm. If a family didn't have several children they might be short-handed. Neither the Winters nor early Davis families had to worry about this. There were ten children in their families.

---

[2] Several pages of transactions involving John Winters are on record in the courthouse in Moundsville WV.

Joshua Winters' World in 1860

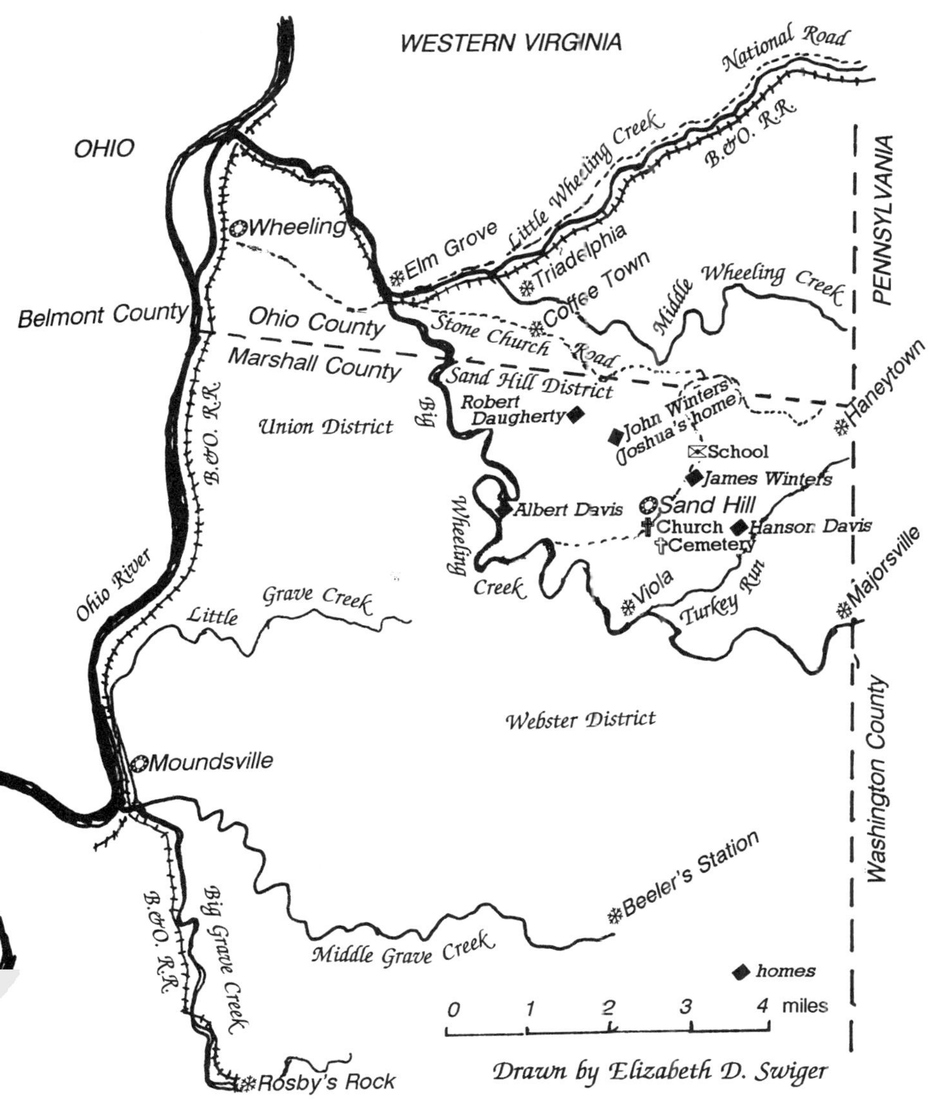

Social events were often associated with work. There were Quiltings, Apple Parings, and Woodchoppings mentioned in the letters by Joshua or his sister, Annie. Others would have included Barn-raisings and Flax Scutchings.[3] Non-work related social activities often involved the Sand Hill Methodist Church, which was a must on Sundays, but they sometimes had "preaching" on other days if there happened to be a travelling preacher in the vicinity. There were Spelling Bees but there is no evidence that Joshua attended. Joshua refers often to *Sings,* which were apparently favorites with young people, and were held in the evening in various churches, community centers, or homes. Then there was always *Visiting.* These were gregarious people who always had the welcome mat out for a relative, friend, or neighbor. A visitor was always urged to stay for a meal.

There was lots of love in these farm family homes, which Joshua reflects constantly. Their family values were well understood and very strong.

Joshua in the Army

In 1861, all ten of the children in Joshua Winters' family were still living at home and ranged in age from eleven to thirty. Joshua had two older brothers and a father to do the heavy work and many sisters for the chores more suited to them. The Civil War had begun and Joshua decided to enlist in the Union Army, the first from his family to do so. He was eighteen. He enlisted for a term of three years in Company G, First Virginia Regiment, Union Volunteer Infantry, on 23 September 1861. Nearly a year later,his two older brothers,Isaac and Alonzo, enlisted in Company I, Fifteenth Western Virginia Regiment,Volunteer Infantry, where Isaac eventually became a 2nd lieutenant and Alonzo a corporal.

---

[3] This writer's father has told her a saying of his grandfather, Isaac D. Winters, (brother of Joshua), when he was older. He might be sitting on the porch, tired after a day's work, and intone with a sigh, "First this world, then the next, then we'll all have to go to a flax-scutching." Apparently it was not a favorite activity of Isaac. It was hot, messy work. As I understand it, the flax was allowed to soak outdoors in a warm solution until the woody part of the flax stock was rotten. Then, in a process called *scutching,* the stalks were beat or scraped to separate the stalks into fibers and remove the waste. It took a long time and was heavy work.

Although Virginia had seceded from the Union and Marshall County was in Virginia, the region was entirely for the Union.[4] Nearly all the young men in Sand Hill District enlisted.[5] Besides Joshua and his two brothers, the future husbands of three of his sisters, a dozen or more of his first and second cousins, and nearly every young man in neighboring households enlisted in the Union forces. During the course of the war, as Joshua's sister Anne noted in her letters, there were few young men around and it was quite lonely. The older men, often suffering from "rheumatism," and the women and girls had to do work formerly carried out by strong young men.

Joshua kept a diary for the entire three years and two months that he served the Union, and wrote to his sisters almost weekly, especially to his next younger sister, Anne Marie (or Anna Maria). The present work consists of the chronological transcription of his writing during his tour of duty. It includes letters from Joshua Winters to his sisters Anna, Kezia, Mary, and Allis (Alice), a few to Joshua from Anna, one to Joshua from his mother, Eliza, and two from Isaac to a sister. The letters are numbered, with diary entries interpolated in proper sequence, so that the entire document is in chronological order.[6]

Joshua was a private throughout his service. His writings give a clear picture of the day-to-day life of a Union foot-soldier, and in his unique phonetic spelling one can almost hear his Western Virginia farm-boy accent. He gets his point across, often with humor. His penmanship is still quite neat and legible and his sentence structure was reasonably correct, but his spelling was "ofell." Either spelling was not a high priority at Sand Hill School in the 1850's, or

---

[4] Although West Virginia dates it's birthday as June 20, 1863, it had been drifting away from the mother state for several years. On Dec 14, 1862, the Sunday New York Herald had an article and map of the new state. Cohen x,xi. At the time of his enlistment, Joshua's regiment was properly called the *First Virginia Regiment*, and at the time of his discharge it was called the *First West Virginia Regiment*. Prior to the official change, the term "Western Virginia" was commonly used.

[5] In the summer of 1862, according to Joshua's letters, there was talk about a draft for the Union Army, and Joshua mentions the possibility several times later. There was no draft when these men enlisted.

[6] The editor has written footnotes to help identify people. Local or family people are identified from genealogical or census data, and military personnel are identified from Civil War reference works.

Joshua himself did not attach much importance to it.

Punctuation is missing entirely and capitalization is sparse in the hand-written letters. To make the account easier to follow, the editor has supplied punctuation. Most of his (lack of) capitalization has been retained, such as his use of a small first-person, i, and his use of lower case letters to begin sentences. He did always capitalize the names of persons, but he was inconsistent with place names. The editor has supplied capitalization for place names if Joshua did not. Spelling is copied verbatim, and at first may be difficult for the reader to follow. If one just pronounces what it says, one will shortly catch on to it. Joshua generally spells words just like he would say them. Portions that could not be read or understood because of faded ink, smudged pencil or folded paper are indicated by square brackets. Any notation made by the editor is either in square brackets or in a footnote.

A map of the area covered by Joshua has been drawn and all place names mentioned in the letters have been labelled. His itinerary was too convoluted to trace but his travels can be followed by referring to the map. The place names are spelled correctly on the map but sometimes Joshua's spelling requires imagination. In especially challenging cases, the correct name may be supplied. When Joshua first went to a region, he would spell the name like it sounded to him, probably not having seen it written. In later references he usually improves, and sometimes eventually gets it right!

Joshua covered the South Branch and Shenandoah Valley regions extensively, as the map indicates. He participated in many skirmishes but his company did not play a major role in any major battle although they were on the outskirts of several. Footnotes identify known skirmishes and battles when he refers to them. Joshua loved the Shenandoah country and often commented on its beauty. "This is shur purty cuntry." He conveyed this love to his son, Mitchell. All his life Mitchell wanted to visit the Shenandoah but he never did.

Joshua's Travels

When Joshua's Company was first deployed in late 1861 he was sent to the Romney area where he was almost immediately involved in a minor but scary enemy engagement. He stayed in the South Branch region most of the winter without incident, and early in the spring of 1862 his company marched into Winchester and proceeded up the Shenandoah Valley (south) and spent the spring traversing the valley, often back and forth. His company moved into the Rapahannock watershed, and in June Joshua was at Manassas and viewed the field where the first battle had been held. In September he was later to participate, peripherially, in the Second Battle of Bull Run, or Manassas. His mother, having heard that his unit had been wiped out in that battle, wrote him a particularly poignant letter when she heard from him that he was safe.[7]

Joshua's two brothers enlisted in the fall of 1862, and apparently Joshua had a leave to go home about that time. He was returned to the eastern panhandle area of (now) West Virginia and spent the winter at North Mountain, without much military activity. His brothers were stationed nearby and he saw them from time to time. The spring of 1863 was spent in the New Creek/Romney/Petersburg region where they engaged in minor skirmishes. They moved up to the North Mountain/Cherry Run vicinity in July as Lee was retreating south after Gettysburg, and back to the South Branch country for the rest of the summer and fall, and were in Petersburg in early December. They made a foray to McDowell, (now in Highland County VA although Joshua didn't know it), and returned to the Petersburg area for the rest of the winter. Joshua noted that he had been serving under (General Benjamin F.) Kelley and had not left West Virginia during the year of 1863. In February 1864 they marched back to New Creek and then went home for a furlough.

The first of April in 1864 saw Joshua's unit returning from home and proceeding toward the Shenandoah Valley again where things were heating up following the Battle of the Wilderness. Company G of the First was close to, or participated in, the battles or skirmishes of Rude's Hill, New Market, Newtown, and Port Republic.

On or about June 5, 1864, Joshua was wounded in the hand, near Staunton VA. He (he said "we") walked the one hundred fifty miles from Staunton VA to Webster WV (near Grafton) where he

---

[7] This letter is on page 45.

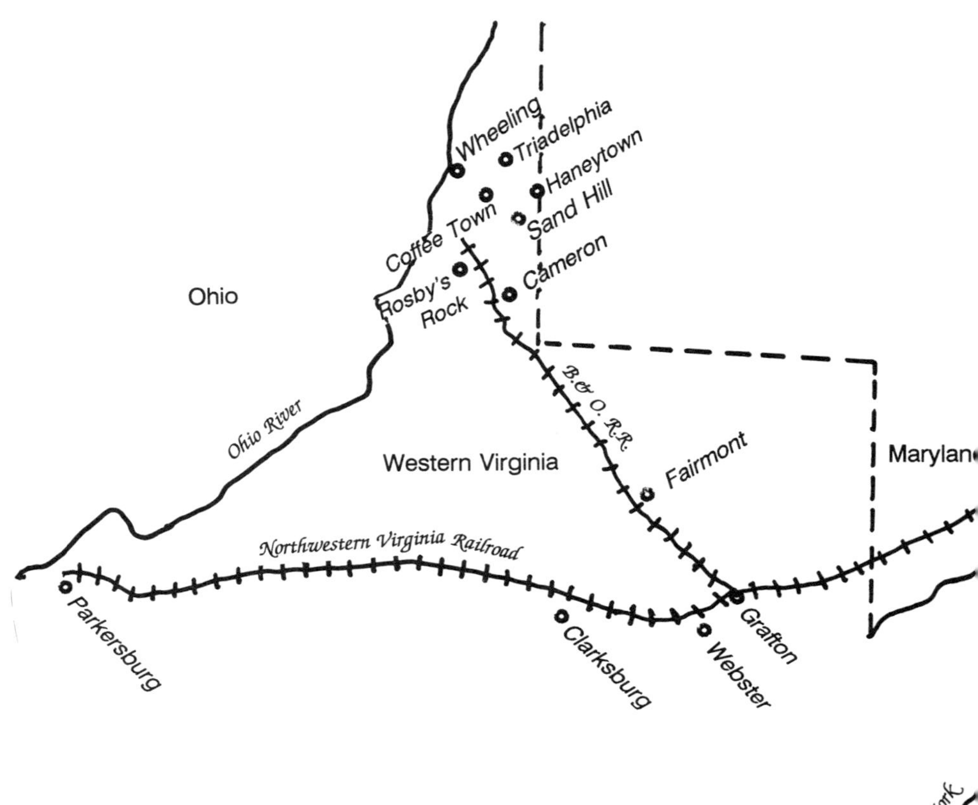

Joshua Winters' Travels in 1861 to 1864

Place Names Mentioned in Letters

Drawn by Elizabeth D. Swiger

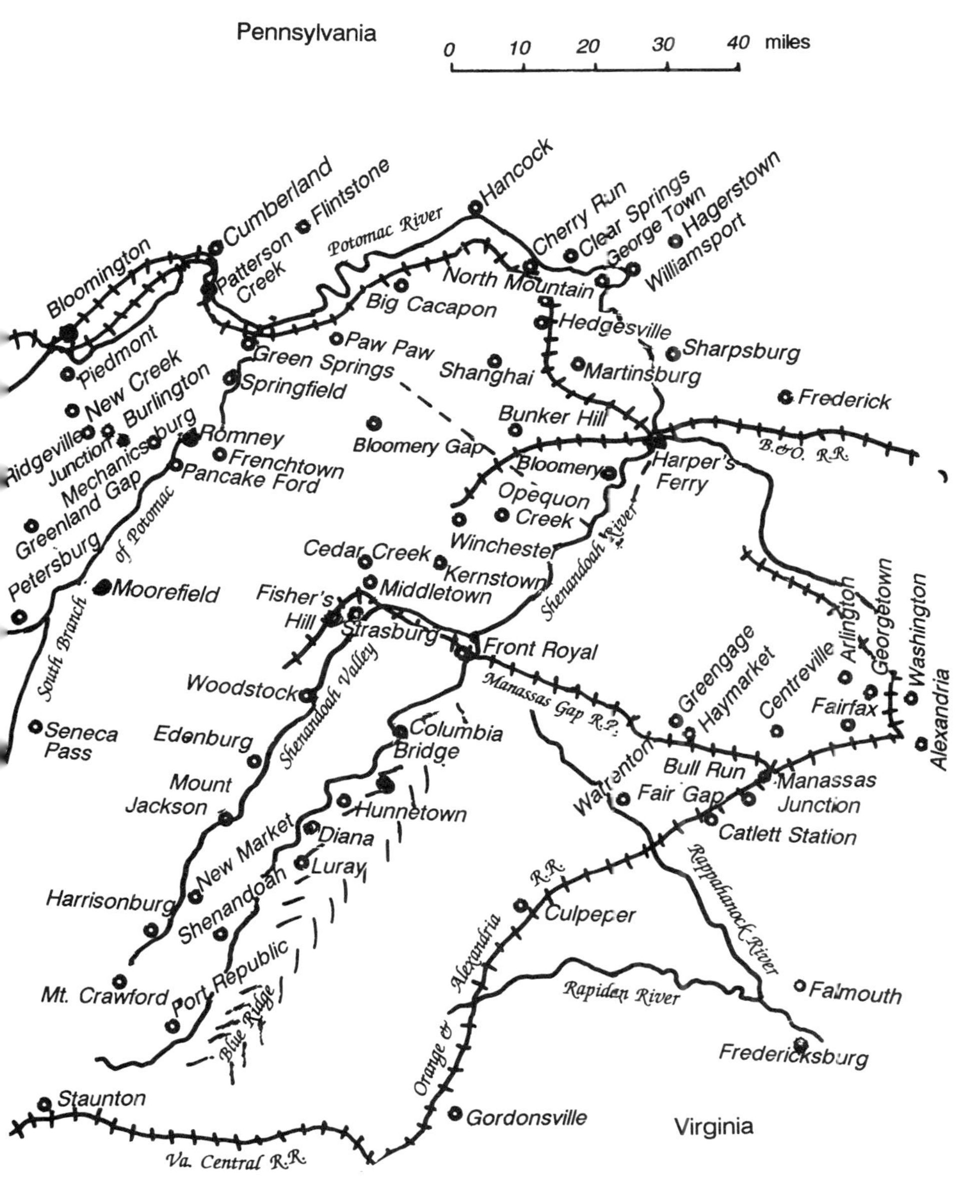

Pennsylvania
0
10
20
30
40
miles
Cumberland
Flintstone
Hancock
Potomac River
Bloomington
Patterson Creek
Cherry Run
Clear Springs
George Town
Hagerstown
Williamsport
North Mountain
Big Cacapon
Hedgesville
Piedmont
Paw Paw
Green Springs
Springfield
Shanghai
Martinsburg
Sharpsburg
New Creek
Burlington
Ridgeville
Junction
Mechanicsburg
Romney
Frenchtown
Pancake Ford
Bloomery Gap
Bunker Hill
Frederick
B.&O. R.R.
Bloomery
Harper's Ferry
Greenland Gap
Petersburg
of Potomac
Opequon Creek
Winchester
Cedar Creek
Kernstown
Middletown
Moorefield
Fisher's Hill
Strasburg
Shenandoah River
South Branch
Front Royal
Woodstock
Shenandoah Valley
Manassas Gap R.R.
Greengage
Haymarket
Centreville
Arlington
Georgetown
Washington
Fairfax
Alexandria
Seneca Pass
Edenburg
Columbia Bridge
Mount Jackson
Hunnetown
Warrenton
Bull Run
Fair Gap
Manassas Junction
Catlett Station
New Market
Diana
Luray
Shenandoah
Harrisonburg
R.R.
Culpeper
Rappahanock River
Alexandria
Port Republic
Mt. Crawford
Blue Ridge
Rapidan River
Falmouth
Fredericksburg
Orange &
Staunton
Gordonsville
Virginia
Va. Central R.R.

got on the railroad and completed the trip to the Parkersburg Hospital and was surprised to find his brother there. He was there most of the summer, and when he was returned to Cumberland to meet up with his unit, he had just missed it. Thus he was sent home for a furlough instead, and was at home during August. When he returned in early September he was sent to the Shenandoah again where he was involved in the Third Battle of Winchester (or Opequon Creek), the Battle of Fisher's Hill and other skirmishes up the valley, lasting until the end of October. On November 12, 1864, three years, one month and twenty days after he had enlisted, Joshua started home for Wheeling. His tour of duty culminated in his discharge on 26 Nov 1864 and Joshua wrote his final note in his diary, "i am free once more."

It seems like a coincidence to the editor that Joshua and his brothers, cousins and other friends in different outfits crossed paths so frequently. Perhaps it is not unusual since they originated in the same area. It was also a surprise to the editor that persons from home sometimes visited the troops. Once two young boys made the trip to visit, once his father visited the brothers, although he missed Joshua, and once Joshua suggested that his sister might make the trip, but there is no evidence that she did.

After the War - Joshua's Family

After the war, Joshua married Beulah Jane Blake, daughter of Joshua and Mary (Cupp) Blake, and raised two children. He lived the rest of his life on the farm that he had inherited from his father when the latter died in 1885.

Their daughter, Laura Effie Winters, was born 16 Oct 1866, and married Albert Downing, son of James and Maria (Grindstaff) Downing. Albert was also descended from early area pioneers. They lived at first in Sand Hill and later moved to the edge of Elm Grove. They had no children, and Laura died in 1942.

Their only son, Mitchell Blake Winters, was born 20 Oct 1869. With only the two children there was lots of work to do on the farm and Mitch worked hard as a young man. In 1896, he married Lucy Grier Davis, youngest daughter of Silas R. and Mary Jane (Davis) Davis. Silas and Joshua were first cousins. Unlike his cousins, Silas had not enlisted in the army but had stayed home and became a prosperous farmer, a fact that did not sit well with some of the Winters' families, but which produced no animosity within Joshua's and Silas' families.

Mitch and Lucy had two daughters: Wilma Waunetta Winters, born in 1902, and Mary Beulah Winters, born in 1904.

Joshua Winters died on 31 May 1900, before the birth of his granddaughters, and was buried in Sand Hill Cemetery, where his tombstone gives his birthdate as 1843.[8] The cause of his death at a relatively young age is unknown to us. His wife, Beulah, and Mitch and Lucy with their daughters continued to live on the family farm for several years, moving into a newly built home in the Elm Grove section of Wheeling in about 1910. Mitchell Winters died Sept 6, 1937.

Wilma Winters married Edward Stevens and lived in Brownsville, PA. They raised a son, Cecil Stevens. Wilma and Ed both died in 1984.

Mary Winters continued to live in the family home with her mother until the latter's death. She is a retired mathematics teacher from Triadelphia High School and lives in Wheeling, WV.

Joshua Winters has only seven living descendants, representing four generations:

1. Mary Beulah Winters, Joshua's granddaughter.
2. Cecil Blake Stevens, Mary's nephew, Joshua's great-grandson.
3. Vicki (Stevens) Felch, Cecil's daughter, Joshua's great-great-granddaughter.
4. Megan Guinti, Lauren Church, Caroline and Jack K. Felch, Vicki's children, Joshua's great-great-great-grandchildren.

No one now living knew Joshua Winters but we know a lot about his personality and character. His writing allows us an insight into his soul. Within or between the lines he wrote to his sister we can experience his inherent decency, his sense of humor, his ethic of hard work and his love for his family and his country. His granddaughter, Mary Winters, has searched her memory for

---

[8] Family records indicate this birthdate which is not consistent with his age as it appears in his discharge, which says nineteen. The Marshall County census records list him as age 8 in 1850, age 16 in 1860, age 25 in 1870 and age 38 in 1880. Joshua himself mentioned his birthday in his diary on January 8, but did not give his age. On 18 Jan 1862 he says "in his twentieth year."

tidbits of information that she had gleaned about her grandfather, who died shortly before she was born. She attests that he was kind, gentle, good-natured and self-disciplined, traits inherited by his son. She remembers her father's cousin[9] speaking of Joshua. He indicated that Joshua was even-tempered with an easy-going disposition, a very friendly, family-oriented man who was glad to see relatives when they visited, and may have wiped a tear from his eye when they left.

Many relatives relate stories of the almost legendary strength of the Winters men, beginning with John and his brother, James, and extending to the sons of both boys. Joshua and his brothers were all over six feet tall, broad-shouldered and physically powerful. Mary relates hearing about Joshua's ability to throw a large sack of grain over his shoulder and run up the stairs to the granary on the second floor of the storage barn on his farm.

Since Joshua and his sister Annie mentioned so many of their uncles, aunts and cousins as well as their sisters and brothers, a pertinent genealogy is included in Appendix B so that the reader can make family connections.

Provenance of the Letters and Diaries

The original letters written by Joshua were kept by his sister, Annie, who never married. She lived all her long life in a house in Sand Hill that she had inherited from her father. She first lived with her sister, Kezia, but after Kezia's death Annie lived alone. In her later years she would visit various nieces and nephews for a week or so at a time. Joshua was apparently her favorite brother, they being so close in age. As she got older she gave Joshua's letters to his daughter, Laura, and maybe even then they were divided and some given to Mitch, but some ended up in the possession of Wilma Stevens of Brownsville PA, granddaughter of Joshua Winters, and when I became interested I borrowed them from my cousin to copy. After Wilma's death in 1984 it was learned that her son, Cecil, had

---

[9] Dr. Earl Roney, son of Beulah (Blake) Winters' sister, Mary, was a dentist who lived and worked in South America. He had probably spent time in Joshua Winters' home after his mother died. His younger brother and sister lived there quite a while.

additional letters and all three of the diaries, which I also borrowed. They were sorted, arranged in chronological order and transcribed into the forerunner of this manuscript. The letters as well as the three diaries belonged to Cecil Stevens of Newport News, Virginia, but he had made them available to me on semi-permanent loan. He has recently presented them to me. It is expected that the original letters will eventually be deposited in the West Virginia University Archives, West Virginia Collection, at Morgantown WV.

Acknowledgements

I wish to thank Mary Winters of Wheeling WV, Cecil Stevens of Newport News VA, and Wilma Stevens, posthumously, for making these documents available to me, and for other help in various ways. The picture of Joshua was provided by Mary Winters and the one of "Aunt Annie" came from Richard L. B. Thomas of Los Angeles, a descendant of Isaac D. Winters. I am grateful to them for these pictures. I thank Alta McNinch of Sand Hill for information about the early town and area, some remembered and some solicited from others.

I acknowledge with appreciation the contributions these friends and colleagues of Fairmont State College:

Robert L. Heffner, Jr., graphics artist, for the cover design. He designed several and it was difficult to choose among them.

D. Stephen Haynes, professor of physics, for background on muzzle-loading rifles that helped explain Joshua's wartime injury.

Wayne Kime and Charles Poston, professors of English, for help in proofreading and editing.

My brother, Wayne Davis of the University of Kentucky, did extensive proofreading and editing on short notice and I thank him. I also appreciate my father, Hannibal Davis, for his interest and memories and my husband, Bill Swiger, for his forbearance.

Elizabeth Davis Swiger
Fairmont, West Virginia

Anna Maria Winters
1845 - 1923

Civil War Letters and Diary

1861

INSCRIPTION IN DIARY:

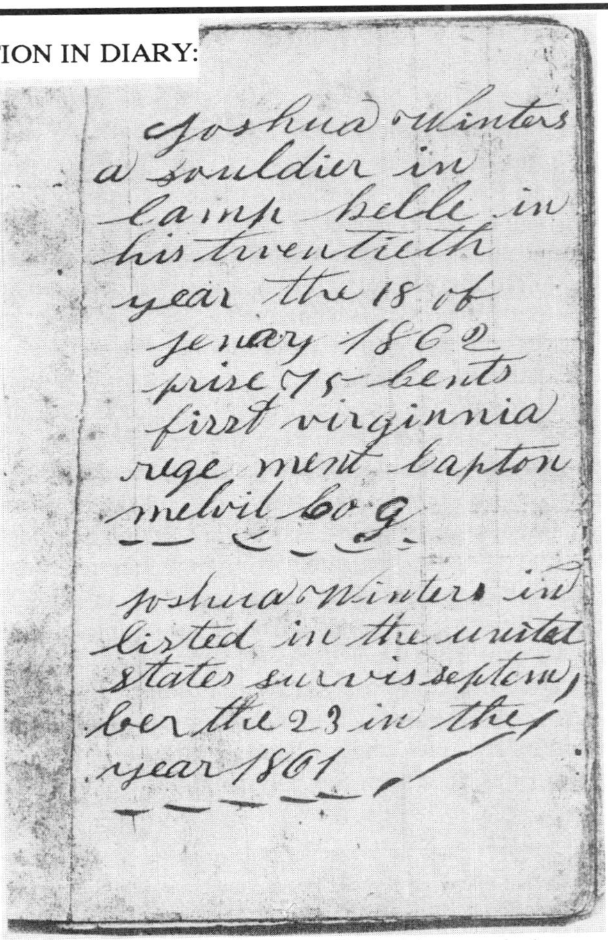
Joshua Winters
a souldier in
Camp Kelle in
his twentieth
year the 18 of
jenary 1862
prise 75 cents
first virginnia
rege ment Capton
melvil Co g.
joshua winters in
listed in the united
states survis septem
ber the 23 in the
year 1861

Joshua Winters, a souldier in Camp Kelle in his twentieth year the 18th of Jenary 1862. Prise 75 cents. First Virginnia regement, Capton Melvil, Co G....... Joshua Winters enlisted in the United States survis september the 23 in the year 1861.

DIARY.[1] Joshua Winters. November 8 1861. we leaft Wheeling November the 8, arive at New Crick the 9, left New Crick on the 9 and went to Burlington. it raind all day, the mud was deap. we staid all night in a stabell. on the 10 we started for Romeny, arived at Romeny at 2 oclock a saboth eaving.

[1] Miss Winters the 12 of November [1861]

Dear sister,

i set down this morning to let you no that i am well at presant and i hope that these fue lins may find you the same. we left Wheeling a Friday and got to New Crick a Satterday about day light. we went out in a bottom and took fence rails and cook our breckfist and i went up on the hill and seen the batery. it is a purty place. we started to Romeny. it was araning. the mud was deap and we went 14 mils to a place calld Burlington. we got thair about dark. we eat our supper and got in a hay mou to sleep. a Sunday morning we started again. we got to Romeny at 2 oclock. we eat our supper and piched our tents. we was tiard the second day. i got my knapsack halld.[2] we ar campt on the outher side of Romeny in a big field on sliden ground. in the morning the sun shins in our tent. we can see Romeny. every regment camps by itself. all the boys is well. it is a purty cuntery. thay shoot 7 and 8 barls every morning. the pickit gard is out 15 mils. the whole cumpeny goes together. thair is a mountain on both sides of us. the name of this camp is Keays. i like it vary well so far. we maid our beds out of spruce pine. we sleep warm. we drill from 9 oclock to 11, from 1 to 3 and dress praid at 4. we waded the crick four times but i didint git mi feet wet. Jacob Soles[3] is cook. when we get in a mile of Fairmont the cars in front of us run off the track and we had to stop and sum of our boys went to a courn huskin. i seen Steve Burkim,[4] at Camuron and he gave

---

[1] Joshua's first diary was a small, pocket notebook with lined pages. In 1863 and 1864 he had pocket diaries with the dates printed with a space to write for each day.

[2] The knapsacks were apparently hauled by horse-drawn wagon, while the troops walked through the mud.

[3] Jacob Soles was apparently a close family friend, but we have no further identity and could not locate him in 1860 census.

[4] Stephen Burkham, physician, age 30, wife Rebecca J. and son Isaac P. M., age 1, were living near Moundsville in 1860 census. Steve is possibly the son of Isaac and

me five plugs of tobacco. i rote to Mary[5] yesterday. tell all the friends to rite soon. giv mi luve to all the friends. no more at presant but remember your brother. this is the way to drect your letters

Joshua Winters
Romeny
Cair of Capton Melvill[5]
First Va regement

we just came off drill. i seen the cavery drill on hourses. Rite soon and tell me all the nuse.

Joshua Winters
to Miss Anny M. Winters

[2]

[about the 12] December 1861

dear sister,

i take up mi pen to night to let you kno that i am well at presant and i hope that these fue lins may find you the same. i recived your letter this eaving. i was glad to git it. our cumpeny and the Co H went out on pickit gard last Sundy morning. [This was Dec 8.] when we got thre mils from camp we hurd that the gards that went out on Satterday and the rebals was a fiting at French town.[7] we throud our over cotes off and started on dobble crick.[8] we went three mils in seventeen minits, but when we got thair the fun was over. the rebbels got in a taun hous [town house] and shot out at our min. thay crippld to and took one of our min. thair was a bout twenty five or thirty of them. we set fire to the taun house and to or three others. thair is one house thair yet but we move in to Romeny. we stod gard till 12 oclock at night then we was clear. in the

---

Nancy (Skiggans) Burkham. If so he was the brother of Melinda Burkham who married Joshua's first cousin, James Franklin Winters, and of Lavisa Burkham Helfenbine who married Joshua's first cousin, Albert G. Davis. Stephen mustered in Co. D, First Regiment on 24 March 1864, deserted in Cumberland 2 June 1865. Powell, 195,199.

[5] Joshua's sister, Mary Ellen Winters.

[6] Captain Oscar F. Melvin.

[7] Called Frenchburg on current maps. Long, 147: Sunday December 8: "Minor skirmish .. broke the Sabbath near Romney."

[8] double quick, or double time.

morning after breckfist our lieutenant and 18 of us went on a scout to mils on the other side of French town. we cum to a old house that was burnt and thair was sum chickings in the fence corner and the lieutenant told us to ketch them, and it wasant long till we had one or to apice. we cut the heads of ov them with our sord banets. then we cum back to that house in Frenchtown. the man had went to Romeny. we got sum more chickings and we went in to the selar and drunk as mutch milk as we cud and we had a grate time of it. it was 3 oclock when we got to camp. we was tired. we ar expecting a fite. the kirnel run us arond a good deal to day on battaling dril. the 7 Ohio regement cum in tonight about dark and the like of holering i never hurd. thair in a nofil site of souldurs hear now and thair is to more regements to be hear tomorrow from indianni. the boys is all well. Dixeson is hear. Seaf and Simpson. Will Hutcherson[9] is well. it is purtty wether hear. i like it first trate. i dount kno when i will git home. i expect in the spring. our capton is at home. i wood like to be at sum of your parteys. well Anne tell all the girls to rite to me. it is a good deal of plasure for me to read them. we sleep warm. thair is five of us in the tent. be shur and tiy gable[10] and make him treat and send me mi shear.

Your brother Joshua

Joshua Winters to
his Sister
Anne M. Winters

---

[9] Cephus Davis (Jr.), James Simpson, William Hutchinson, and William Dickson or Dixon. "Seaf" Davis, Joshua's second cousin, was mustered into Co. K, First Va. on 14 Nov 1861, age 21. Powell, 203. William Dixon, age 26, was mustered into Co. L of the Sixth Va. on 12 Nov 1861. Powell, 207.

[10] What this means is unknown.

DIARY. Jenuary the 10 1862. we left Romeny at dark, travel all night, the mud was vary deap. we arived at Springfield on the 11, leaft thair on the 11, arived at Patterson Crick on the 11. Camp Kelley. arive thair at dark. it was a vary muddy march and we was vary tired. we left Camp Kelley Febuary the 5 in the morning and arived at Camp Steel Cross rodes the 5 at three oclock in the eaving and staid thair till midnight, then went six mils, halted about nine in the morning, staid thair till four in the eaving, then returnd back to Camp Steel. that was a purty march. the snow was about nine inches deap, the rodes was good. we left Camp Steel on the 13 and cum to camp in the woods on the 13. it was a purty day overhead but muddy.

[3] Jenery the 15 1862

dear sister,

it is with plazure that i take mi pen in hand to let you no that i am well at presant and i hope that these fue lins may find you injoying the same blessin. well Anne we have left Romeny last friday the 10 of jenery. the Capton cum around at one oclock a friday morning, told us to git up and git reddy to march. i tell you we got up in a hurry, got our breckfist and was reddy to start at daylight but we didint start till at night. our Conel made a speach. he told us that thair was glory a head but we haint sean it yet. when we went to start our Capton told us he didint no where we was a goin and all he had to say to Co G was to stick to him and when he run for us to run but he didint think he wood run. the wagons was all a head of us and we had to go vary slo. we marchd till four oclock in the morning. we got to Springfield, we stopd a while then we started again. we got to Frankford at diner time, started again to Patterson Station. we got hear about four oclock. we was purty tired when we got hear. we ar hear yet. our camp is two mils from hear. we ar expectin to go every day. thair was about 9 thousand of us. it was araining. you might know how muddy it was after all them a goin. the mud was a running off the rode. in sum places it was over boot tops. we had sum of the biggist fires a cuming I ever saw. we started a friday night at seven and got hear a satterday at four in the eaving and it is onely ninteen mils. you may no how slo we cum. we are in eight mils of Cumberlent rite besides the rail rode. i was a riding up and down the rail rode yesterday a fixin it sose we cud git to our Camp. it snode and sleated hear last night and today we got paid off. i got four letters a littel bit ago. i will anser them as soon as i cin. i like this place furstrate. the boys is all gittin boots today. if i had mine halfsold that wood last me to spring. Dirict your letters to Camp Kelley, Hampshire Co Va first va regement Capton Melvil Co G. John is well and all the rest of these boys. no more at presant but remember your brother. rite soon.

Joshua Winters to Anne M. Winters.
rite soon excuse mi bad riting.

[4] Jenary the 31 1862

Dear sister,

it is with plazure that i sit down to let you no that i am well at presant and i hope these fue lins may find you the same. i recive your letter today and i was glad to hear from you. we ar still at Patterson Crick. it is the muddiest place i ever saw. the lieutenant is in our tent. he cums to our tent purty ofen and stays awhile. thair is sixteen of us in one tent. we hav a stove in the middle and we git along furstrate at night. when we all get acutting up we have a grate time. i hav onely bin on gard once since we cum hear. thair is an offul site of men hear now and more a cuming. we hav all bin bizzy this fore noon gittin brush and putting it before the tent sose we woodant swamp in the mud. wenzdy our regement went out to capture sum things. we went on the cars[11] to Springfield. our Co and Co B got off thair and started on the Romney rode. we went about six mils then we cum back. we wood of went further but that was further than the Conell told us to go. we was in 5 mils of two regements of Secesh.[12] Mager Devoill[13] was with us. the Curnell went with the rest down the rail rode further. they got about two

[11] On the railroad.

[12] "Secesh" was Joshua's word for the secessionists. Sometimes he called them rebels, but only once did he speak of them as "the eneme."

[13] Isaac H. Duval was from Brooke County WV. He was a major in the First WV, later a colonel in the Ninth WV and eventually a Brigidier General. Cohen, 10.

thousands bushell of corn and rie. we got back at nine at night. when we drill we haf to go two mils. the other day thair was four thousand of us out in one field and we all started across the field on a baynet charge and every man a hollerin his best. if you had bin a lissning you might of herd us. the boys is all well. Sam[14] got to go home at last. he has bin triying to go a good while. i wood like to go to sum of the sinings[15] at Sand Hill. thair is no sine of us a leaving hear. I haint seen Will Marsh[16] or Jolius[17] since the next day after we cum hear. thair camp is over the river about a mile from hear. i think i will go over be fore long to sea them. the boys is all laying around the tent a reading and sleeping. all you do hear is eat and sleep and stand gard once a week or so. i cant think of enne thing more to rite and the mail will leave in a fue minits and i am that lazy i cant rite enne more. no more at presant but remember your brother till death. i send my luv to all you and all inquirin frends if enne thair be. rite soon. excuse mi bad riting and spelling and for not riting more. rite soon and tell me all the nues.

Miss Anne M. Winters from Joshua Winters. rite soon.

DIARY. Febuary the 2 1862. this is sabath day. i am on picket gard three mils from Camp Kelley in a vallee. thair is three of us. we can see Frankford. it is a purty day. the sun is a shining. it snode hard last night. the countersine was Yourk.[18]

---

[14] We don't know who Sam is. Samuel W. Kimmins who married Joshua's cousin, Matilda Mooney, was the same age as Joshua. He was in the Co D, First Reg but did not enlist until 12/62. Powell, 195. Other Samuels in Joshua's company included McCoy, McCann, and Nangle.

[15] A sing, or a singing, was a social meeting, sometimes at a church but usually at someones house, a school or a community center. It was characterized by group singing, usually hymns but not always, refreshments and socializing, but no dancing. Joshua and his sister both always spelled it "sining," but it didn't denote sinning. Apparently it was a socially acceptable way for young men and women to get together.

[16] 1860 Marshall County census near the Winters family; Abraham Marsh, age 67, Eliza, age 55, William, age 22. The Marsh families had close connections with the Winters' families.

[17] We don't know who "Jolius" is. Joshua never mentions his last name.

[18] A password given to the "picket gards"to let them know you were friend, not foe.

[5] Satterday the 15 [February] 1862

Dear sister,

it is with plazure that set down to let you no that i am well at presant and i hope these fue lins will find you all the same. i got your letter last eaving and i was glad to hear from home and that you ar all well. i rote mother a letter the other day. i recon she will hav a grate time a reding it. i rote it with a led pencel. mi knapsack wasant thair. i thout maby you coud read sum of it. we left Camp Cross Rodes a thirsday and cum hear. i dont no what thay will call this place. we ar 2 mils of the rail rode, 2 mils from Paw Paw on a hillside in the woods. we had to clear a place to put our tent on. when we left Patterson Crick we left our tents thair and knapsacks but we got them to day. we was without them ten days. thair was a littell fight ten mils from hear yesterday at Blumington Gap.[19] thay killed 25 or 30 and took 50 priseners. the most of them was ofisors. thair was 2 of our Cavery killed. Sam has not got hear yet. he had better cum back soon. the boys is all well. Will Marsh was hear a littell bit a go. he has got a vary bad cold. he says Jolius is in the hors pittell.[20] i wood like to bea on Sand Hill when you wood hav the exbeshon. i wood like to of seen you and Mary Frances on the old bay when you got throde off. i wood like to of been at home when Harvey[21] cum with her. i think i wood of had sum fun with them. i will finish it tomorrow.

Sunday the 16 1862. Well Anne you tell Isaac[22] that Will Marsh rote 2 letters to him and he wants him to rite to him. well go to all the parteys that you can. rite soon and tell me all the noos. well i cant think of enne thing more. no more at presant but remember your brother till death.

---

[19] I think Joshua means Bloomery Gap. Bloomington was in the other direction. According to Cohen, 34, on Feb 14 1862, Federal forces attacked Confederates at Bloomery Gap in Hampshire County and routed them. They fled towards Winchester but returned as soon as the Federals returned to their camp at Paw Paw.

[20] hospital.

[21] William Harvey Winters, Joshua's first cousin. He married Maria Minor. Mary Frances is unknown.

[22] Joshua's oldest brother, Isaac Davis Winters. He is the great-grandfather of the editor.

Joshua Winters to Miss Anne Winters. Good by. rite soon. tell Nancy[23] i will rite to hur in a day or to. giv mi luv to all the inquiren frends if enne thair be. drect your letters to First Virginia regement Co G in cair of Capton Melvill.

DIARY. March the 11 1862. left Camp Woods at four in the eaving, went 8 mils. we crossd Big Capon on a bridge of wagons, staid thair till three the next day, then returnd back to Camp again on the count of Generl Landres death. third begaid Gen Shields.[24] we left Camp Paw Paw March the 8 1862, got in the cars in the morning and the morning of the 9 we was on the rail rode a piece. we staid thair awhile and battel sung and praid then we started and got to Cherry Crick at dark, then to Bacon Crick. the bridg was burnt, the track tourn up. we staid thair till the 11 of March, then shouldered our knapsacks and marched on the railrode to Martainsburg, 12 mils. camped all night in a vary purty place. On the morning of the 12 we started on a force march on Crick time.[25] we got in three mils of Winchester, halted in a big level field. we went 18 mils that day. all about give out.

[6] March the 15th 1862
Camp near Winchester

Dear sister,

i take my pen in hand to let you no that i am well at present and i hope if these few lins reach you thay may find you in good helth. Well Anne we left Paw Paw the 8 of March, got on the cars in the morning, that was satterday, and a sunday morning we was at Hancock. We staid there till after dinner but [?] reach thair on the platform, then we cum to Cherry Run, staid thair a nowhor or to,[26] then we cum to Bacon Creek, got thair asunday night about 9 oclock. i staid all night with Will Marsh. Well we staid thair till

---

[23] Susan Nancy Winters, Joshua's sister.

[24] James Shields, Brigidier General in charge of volunteers in Virginia after General Frederick W. Landers died. He fought Jackson at Kernstown and at Port Republic. Strother, 7.

[25] Quick time, usually called double time now.

[26] an hour or two.

tusday then we started on foot. the bridge was toirn down and 5 miles of the railrode was tor up and we had to footit and kire our knapsac. we cum 10 miles this side of Martainsburg that day, 12 miles, camp thair that night. Martainsburg is a pretty place and sum of the prettiest girls thair i ever saw. when the war is over i could liv thair. well a wessday morning we left every thing but our haversachs and overcotes and started on a good hike and a force march. Three of Ohio was before us and thay like to wore us down but thay coudant do it. [several lines too faded to read] and gard all of the ground. i was tiard. we went on to [Cold?] Crick. [we war a c hilly mies] and halted in a big field in three miles of Winchester. When we hurd that Banks[27] had took Winchester we stopped. he took it without ever firing one gun. when he was goin in one end of the town they was goin out the other end. i gess thay hav all left Manasses and are at Strassburg that is 15 or twenty miles on the other side of Winchester. Thair is no boddy can tell how menne soulders is in Winchester and along this rode. thair is so menne thay are aplain back and fords with canans. yesterday thay throu shells at one another. we take sum prisiners every day. thay was a fiting out thair today. we cum near the canans vary plain but we dont git to see enne of the fun. well we are in the gardin of the world. it is levell and pretty country and tall bildings and pretty girls. this is the place i could liv. well the boys is all well but John Cruson.[28] he took sick at Paw Paw [can't read fold in page] brick and is thair yet and one more of our min and sum more. thair is a doctor with them. i hurd this eaving that he was vary bad. i recon he will go to the hors pittel. Jake is well and i am as well as i ever was. i think the war will be over and all of us at home aginst this time next year. we drill a good deal now. it rain all day today. i recon you will have a good time at Isaac's. well i wood like to be at home at it but i like it better than ever since i got out in this pretty place. it is gittin late and i must quit. i could rite to or three sheets but it is late, no more

---

[27] Nathaniel P. Banks, from MA where he had been Governor, commanded the Department of the Shenandoah in 1862. At his approach to Winchester on March 11, 1862, Jackson and 4600 men withdrew and were followed southward up the valley by Bank's command. Long, 183.

[28] 1860 Marshall County census, Fair Hill P. O.; John Crusan, age 60, wife Margaret, 58, John 19 and Rachel 15. John G. Cruson was in Co. E, First Regiment. Powell, 201. Spelling as given in sources.

at present. rite soon and rite a big letter. direct your letters to Capton Melvill Co, First Va regiment, infantry, east of Cumberland.

Joshua Winters to Anne M. Winters,

rite soon excuse me for not riting for it is late, good night.

DIARY. Frederick Co 1862. March the 18. we left Camp Shield for Strawsburg. we went to Seder Crick the first day, fired on thair rear gard, staid thair all night, started the next morning and attacked them on the other side of Strawsburg. sheld then staid that night thair. the next day we returned to Camp again. it raind. it was a hard march. vary tired. March 29 1862. we left Camp Shields March the 23. got three mils from Winchester then had a fite 4 in the eaving.[29] staid thair all night. in the morning we started after them, got to Ceder Crick, staid all night. the next morning we followd them to Strawsburg, camp thair. we was firin canons at them every mile or to Camp Kimbell.

[7]

March the 30th 1862
Saboth eaving
Camp Kimbel JW AMW

Dear sister,

it is with plazure that i set down this Saboth eaving to let you no that i am well at presant and i hope these few lins will find you all in good helth.

well Anne i received your letter this morning and i was glad to hear from you. it has bin wet hear for to or three days. the 23, that was last sunday we left Camp at dinertime,got to Winchester. we heard the canon and we went to mils futher.then we stopped and all regements scatterd. we went on a littel futher and stopped and when the canon balls whisselled over our heads you ott to of seen us a dodgin. we all cum down in one motion. then we turnd back and all got together, laid our cloth off[30],went throu the fields

[29] On March 18, a skirmish at Middletown VA, on March 19 one at Strasburg, and on Sunday March 23 the Battle of Kernstown was fought just south of Winchester. Jackson retreated south up the valley. Total casualties were Jackson, 718, Federals, 590. Long, 186-188.

[30] Writing very legible, meaning unclear. Probably bedroll, tents, blankets, etc.

a mile, got in the woods. first our brigaid got in a colem and our Co and Co A started out to schrimish. we scatterd throu the woods. we got a littel piece when thay shot at us but shot too hi. then it commenced. it was about four in the eaving and till night it was a continual row. our kirnel put his cap on his sord and started throu the field and he holard Com on Boys. he got shot. thay was behint the stone fence. we lost a grate menne min but thay lost four to our one. Co A and our Co fired the first shot. we didant lose a man. the balls flue thick. the next morning we took after them. we looked in 10 mils of the raid. goin throu the wheat fields the mud wood stick to us. we got to Cedar Creek that day. at night our Co had 12 min. all the rest giv out. we got close anuf to fire the canon.[31] [End of first page, both sides. Next page missing.]

DIARY. Aprile 1 1862. Left Camp Kimbell Aprile the first, went 17 mils then stop on a count of the bridg being burnt. it was warm. we was close anuf to holler at them. Camp in the woods beside the pike. Camp Devall, Shanandore Co.

[8] Aprile the 15 1862

Dear sister,

it is with plazure that i take mi pen in hand to let you no that i am well at presant and i hope these fue lins will find you all the same. well Anne i recived your letter to day and i was glad to get it but sorrow to hear that Alle[32] was sick but i hope that she is well by this time. well Anne thair aint much noos to rite. it has bin a raining all day. we had a revew hear last week. all of Genearl Shields devishin got in one big field. he rode out in a buggy. it was a big croud of peapell. yesterday thair was a gennerl in spection. ever thing is quiet to day. no noos onely general Tilar[33] says we will

[31] This would be the Kernstown battle Joshua is describing. Jackson had 3500 men and struck hard but Shields had 900, well in place. Although the battle was decisive and the opening of the Shenandoah Valley Campaign, Joshua overestimated the opponents losses, or underestimated those of his side. Long, 188. [Too bad the last page of this letter is missing.]

[32] Alice Eliza Winters, Joshua's youngest sister.

[33] Brig. General Erastus Bernard Tyler.

never go enne further but i dont belive him.

well have hurd sum good noos this last week. well we got paid off. i would like to be at home to help Lol plow. John Cruson has got abell to sing and dance again. Jake is well. thair is no more sine of a fite hear than thair was 2 weeks ago. i rote to Lonzo[34] and to you. the letters shure dont go well. i want to rite Nance a fue lins so i will bring yours to a close. i recon you hurd of Fourt Sumptor bein takin, John Brown bein hung, Zola Croffer bein dead, Linkin bein lected president, South Carolina goin out of the union and all sutch late noos as this. nuthing more at presant but still remember your brother Joshua Winters.

to Miss Anne M. Winters. rite soon.

Give my luv to all inquiren frends if enne thair be. Good by but i hope not for long. rite soon.

DIARY. Aprile the 30 1862. we left Camp Thoburn Aprile the 30 at 2 oclock in the eaving, march 14 mils, halted near Columban Bridg 8 oclock at night. it raind that night. Crossd the mountain into Page Co. May the 7. we went out to renforce the 13 Indianna 4 mils from Columban bridge. went to dubell Crick, return to the bridg at dark. our Co went on picket at Hunnetown.[35] Staid on gard five days.

[9]

May the 9 1862
Camp near Columbinan Bridg

Dear sister,

it is with plazure that i rite you these fue lins this warm eaving to let you no that i am well at presant and i hope this letter will find you all the same. Well Anne i rote you a letter this week. i told you about us a goin out and the Seasesh a trying to surround us in Diannia. Sayed we got scared for nuthing but thay tride it and got anuf. Thay lost sum men, got around one Co of our Cavery but thay swum the river, got off safe. our regement went out on dubell Crick

[34] Alonzo Winters, Joshua's brother, also called Lol.

[35] The editor could not locate Hunnetown or Honeytown so estimated its location on the map on pages 14-15.

to help them but we met them a cumin in. we turnd back, cum to the bridg, and our Co cum up the river on gard.[36] we have bin out hear to day. we have a good place. i wood just as leav be out hear as in Camp. we was a looking for them last night. we bilt a fence across the rode to keep the Cavery back but thay didint cum. our Cavery went out to day. thay have left. we ar a goin to leav. our tents is gone. the Kirnell says we have one hundred mils to go. i recon it is to Richmond. our men is thair now.

i am on gard and 8 more of us. thair is three or fore of us a riting. the boys is all well. John has bin all through the cuntery to day. he got sum bred. thair is plenty of girls hear. thay ar union and vary frendly. i will quit for tonight. i must git mi supper. i will finish tomorrow.

May the 10 1862. Satterday the 10. i set down this morning to finish your letter. i am off of gard. we got along furstrate last night. thair was a weding hear this week. the girl lives hear. he lives outside of our pickets. he cudint get in but she went out to her unkells and got maired yisterday. thay discharged all the old men and all the sick. the hole army is on the move. it looks like it wood soon be over. i guess i had better quit for you will have a grate time reading this letter. drect your letters the same way. Joshua.

DIARY. Wednesday May the 14. raind all day. march on. got to Frunt Royal 4 oclock p m. all of Shields devision thair. camp thair all night. Thursday the 15. on our march again. our regement ahead. crost the Blue Ridge. still raind. went to scirmisching as soon as we cross the ridg. the Cavery in sight. camp in the rain all night. May the 16 1862, friday. still rains. 7 Ohio in advance, our regement in the rear. Rebell Cavery made thair appearence at Cross Rodes. we fired at them and marched on. Camp in the woods. Satterday the 17. bieautifull day but muddy. started at 6 oclock on our march. at 6 in the eaving our begaid[37] marcht through Warrenton in advance with Colours a flying, drums a playing. Camp in a mile of that place. it is a nice place. Sunday the 18. beautiful weather. laid over thair all

---

[36] On May 5 there was fighting at Columbia Bridge. Long, 207.

[37] We assume the reader knows by now that when a begaid scirmisches that a brigade skirmishes.

day. the 1st and 2" begaid past us that day. i went to church. Munday may the 19. cloudy, cool. started on our march again at 6 in the morning. our begaid in the rear, vary slo, ketch up to the rest at one oclock. Camp in a nice bottom at Catilon Station. we was 8 days a cumon from Columblin Brige hear, about 100 mils. we had bad rodes, wet wether, hard marchin. this is beautiful cunttery.

[10] May the 20 (1862)
Fauquer Co

Dear sister,

i set down this eaving to let you no that i am well at presant and i hope this will find you all the same. well Anne i got the fue lins you sent me in Kezias[38] letter. i got it last eaving. i will send this by Seaf Davis. the letters i send by mail dont go i dont think. i rote you one when i was on picket at Columbinia Brige. i put sum seasesh munne[39] in it. i want to no if you got it or not. we left thair the 12 of May. that was munday. we marcht till satterday, got to Warrnton a satterday, staid thair till munday, then started and got hear amunday eaving. we had five days rain on our march, sum vary muddy rodes. we cum purty fast sum times. we seen 500 seacesh Cavery at Cross Rodes but we soon made them travell. we seen sum purty cuntery after we crost the Blue Rige. Warrnton is the purtiest place we hav seen yet. we ar at Catlet Station in 40 mils of Washington cittee. we dont expect to stay hear long. all of Shields deveshin is hear. Will Marsh is hear. he is well. Jolius is below Harpers Farry. we haint hurd from him for a good while. all the rest of the boys is well. thair is a good menne soulders hear. when we cum in thay thout we was hard looking fellows. thay ar just from Washington. we call them sunday soulders. thay told us that thay had sum hard times. thay say thay hav bin on gard one night when it raind and was 2 nights without thair tents. thay think it is offul hard and thay had to eat crackers to day for the first time. i think if thay follow us awhile thay can hav sumthing to talk about. we dont no whare we will go. thair is no important noos as i no of. well i recon Lonzo has got his corn planted. Thay aint done out here yet. well i cant think of mutch to rite as i am vary lazy. drect your letters to

[38] Kezia Winters was Joshua's oldest sister.

[39] Confederate money.

Fredericksburg. we have no tents but the kirnell giv us his fly that he puts over his tent. it just holds what was in our tent. it keeps us dry but the rest of them has to git under thair blankets. no more at presant. giv mi luv to all the frends. rite soon. good by. i will rite in a fue days again. i gess Seaf[40] will go to morrow. good by but i hope not for long. tell al of the frends to rite. i gess this is Fauquer Co. drect your letters to Frederick, First Va infantery regement.

Joshua Winters to Miss M Winters
Sand Hill Marshall Co Va

DIARY. Wenzy May the 21 1862. we left Cattlet Station 9 oclock in the morning, marcht vary slo till dark then went vary fast till seven at night. we was vary tired. our begaid in the rear. purty wether. Camp beside the rode. went 14 mils. Thursdy May the 22 1862. on our big march again, warm, rodes durty. we hav stopt for diner in the woods. our begaid in the rear, our regement in the advance. we went through Falmout Camp in one mile to the left of Fredericksburg. a vary purty place. May the 25, Sunday. purty day. started on our march again, back to Catlett Station. we went 6 mils, camp all night. May the 26. started again. we reach Catlett Station at night. we went fast. we marcht 20 mils. we was tired. grate excitement all night. Wenzy the 28 th May 1862. we left Catlett Station at 2 oclock in the eaving, went through a littell vilage by the name of Greangage, camp 2 mils abov Haymarket. went 12 mils. May the 29 1862. beautiful day, roads dusty on our march. again went through white plains camp in a mile of rector town Camp at 3 in the eaving. got our supper then started again. marcht all night over rough rodes. we hav stopt for breckfist in the woods. we ar all tired and sleepee. May the 30 1862. on the road again. our regement in the rear of the begaid, our Co bringing up the straglers. warm marching. halted for diner. raining hard. start again. went 19 mils. camp at Frunt Roial. heard thunder storm at dark. all vary tired and wet. May the 31 1862. Clouddy morning. wating for marching orders. got them at 12 oclock. started on a reconnisens. went 4 mils when the shells flue around us purty thick. we deploid schrimmishers. our canons soon started, then we follored them three mils then returned to camp.

---

[40] Cephas Davis.

June the 1 1862. on our march again back to Luray. started at twelve, went 10 mils. camp in the woods. heavy thunder storm at dark. out of grub. vary hungree. June the 2 1862. on our march again. raining, rodes muddee, reached Luray 4 oclock. went on the other side and campt in the woods. went 17 mils that day, all wet and tired. heavy thunder and litning. June the 4 1862. on our march again. started from Luray before breckfist. went 10 mils, got our breckfist and started again. went 5 mils further then stop. the rodes so bad we coudant go enne further. raining hard, the mud and water nee deap. we was tired wet and muddee ......Satterday the 7 1862. on our march again. started in the morning, marcht up the Shanandore river. stopped at Furre Furnace for diner then marcht till 9 at night. June the 8 1862. on our march again. started one in the morning, march 12 mils. in site of the enemee. commenced shelling. we fell back in the woods, laid thair all night beside the run. June the 9 1862. canonaiding commenced erlee in the morning. the muskits at 7 1/2. hard fiting. fell back 16 mils, staid all night.[41] June the 10 1862. on our march again. got to the Columban Bridg at dark. rodes muddee, rain all day, hard marching. June 11 1862. on our march again. went 9 mils. Camp on the other side of Luray. rodes muddee in a purty place.

[11]

Thirsday Luray Virginia
June the 12th 1862

Dear sister,

i set down once more to let you no that i am well at the present time and i hope these few lines will find you all injoying good helth. well we haint been in one place long anuf to git the mail but i still sent a letter every chance i got. the maill will git here to day and i will expect to get to or three from home. we hav bin goin backwards and fords for to munts. last Sunday we met old Jackson[42] at Fort Publick up the Shanadore River. he was on the outher side of the river. thair was only 4 regements of us, it is call

[41] These battles, described in more detail in the next letter, were known as the Battles of Cross Keys and Port Republic, and were fought on June 8 and 9. They are considered to be the last battles of Jackson's Shenadoah Campaign. Long, 224.

[42] General Thomas "Stonewall" Jackson, Confederate, from Western VA.

the 4 begaid, but Jackson soon shell us back. then Freemont[43] commenced on the outher side. they haltit that evening. the third begaid cum up to help us. Jackson cross the river a sunday night, amunday morning the fite commenced. we drove them back on the bottom but thay got in the mountain and cum in behint us on our canans. we had to fall back betwean them and the river. that got to of our canans. we lost a good menne min but thay lost more then we had in the fight. we retreated back that day 14 mils then the rest of Generl Shealds devishen met us. we staid thair that night then com back to mils this side of Luray. we lost 4 min out of our Co and three slightly wounded. thay say Freemont crost the river that eaving and whip Jackson, burnt his train and camp on the battel ground. i hope it is so but i don't no whair it is or not. i neadn't tell you enne more about it. you will see it in the papers. well Jake and Sam is in the hors pittel before the fight but i gess thay aint vary bad. John Cruson and Will Marsh is well. Jake has just cum to camp. he is well now. Anne the chirrees is ripe out hear. i still liv in hopes of gettin home this fall to git sum appels. this is a vary pretty place. Seaf is gon home at least. He has a letter for you. it has bin rote for a long time. rite and tell me all the noos and who goes with all the girls and how [Harioll?] is getin along. oh how i wood like to see you all once more and go to Sand Hill meeting house but i hope it wont belong till i am home. tell Lonzo to rite. i recon he is bizze at the corn. tell me how mom's lag is this spring. giv mi love to all them and to all inquiren frends. no more but still remain your loving brother.

Joshua Winters to Anne Winters
direct your letters to Luray. good by rite soon.

DIARY. June the 15 1862. we left Luray 9 oclock in the morning, marcht 10 mils. Camp in the woods. vary warm. raind a shower. packed our knapsacks. Capton Wedall in command. June the 16 1862. on our march again early in the morning in light marching order. went 15 mils. campt at Frunt Roial in a nice field. warm weather. June the 19 1862. we left Frunt Roial at dark. got on the

[43] John Charles Fremont was in charge of the Department of the West early in the war but was commanding the Union troops in Western VA at this time.

cars. got to Manasses at daylight. Camp between thair and Catlett Station till the regement got in. we had sum vary hard storms thair. the regement got thair the 22and campt all night and on the 23 we moved our camp. on the 24 we had a generel in spection.

[12] June the 23 1862
Manassess Junction

Dear sister,

it is with plazure that i set down this morning to let you no that i am well at presant and i hope these fue lins will find you all in joying good health. well Anne i got a letter from you the outher day. we left Frunt Roial last friday night and got hear a satterday morning. thay told us all that didint feel abell to march hear to get on the cars and thair was about 90 of our regement got on. Thair was 15 of our Co rode hear. thay told Shealds that he could get cars for all his divishin but he said his men coud walk. we thout it was as easy to ride when we coud git the chance as to walk. this is munday. we hav bin hear three days. i think the regement will git hear tonight. we have a good time hear. it is a levell place. the train runs through our camp. we ar between Catlet Station and the Junction. we can get on the cars and go enne place. we hav nuthing to do hear but drink lemon aid and beer, eat cherries, read the noos, and fish. i dont care if the rest dont git hear this sumer. thair is sum out of all regements and begaids. i recon thair is two or three regements all together. i dont no whare we ar a goin to from hear. it is hard to tell. everything is quiet now. we are expection to hear every day about Macclenin[44] fiting at Richmond.

well Anne i hurd that thair is to be a selabration at Sand Hill the fourth of July. i hope you will hav a good time for me and giv my best respects to all the purty girls. no more at presant. cant send it till the regement gits hear and i will hear more news then. i will send it then.

June 24. well the regement got hear last eaving, a munday eaving, when we was eating our supper in the Captons tent. thair was an offul storm. we got aholt of the tent and held on like death to a nigger. we had another storm last eaving. i seen the battell ground at Manassess Junction. i like this place vary well. i dont no

[44] General George B. McClellan.

how long we will stay hear. all the boys is well at present. well Anne i rote to Lib and Jim[45] but i gess thay wont anser it. i rote to Easter[46] the outher day. i am in good health and i hope these fue lins find you the same. rite and tell me what kind of a time you had the fourth and tell me how you and Capton Black[47] is agittin along and all the noos. Drect your letters to the First Va regement infantry in cair of Capton Melvil, Shealds devishin and i gess thay will cum enne how. no more at presant but still remain your brother.

Joshua Winters to Miss Anna M. Winters.

giv mi luv to all and rite soon. i cant think of enne thing more now. will rite soon again. the boys had a purty hard march hear but i had a easy time. i rode on the cars.

Joshua Winters.

Good by but i hope not for long, not for ever.

DIARY. June the 27 1862. me and Richard Ball[48] has bin on the battell ground at Bulls Run to day and in the forts. we left camp in the morning and got back at dark. thay got marching orders and all packed up reddy to start when we got back. got on the [cars] at 10 oclock. got into Elezandria at day light on the 28. Camp in town till eaving, then moved out three mils, camp that night. On the 29 we moved our campground again in a beautiful place. then me and Calvin Coury[49] went to see the forts, and on the 30 we musterd out for pay. vary warm to day. i spent the 4th in camp, vary lonsom. it is vary warm.

July the 18 1862. it is cloudy to day. i was at a speaking to night at camp. Saterday the 19. beautiful day. we ar bizzy this morning a fixing our street. i washed mi shirts this eaving. all gay and happy tonight. the fiddling and dancing is going on on our street to night. Sunday the 20. beautiful day. we was out on revew this morning. we was on revew this eaving again. it is warm. Munday the 21. nice day.

---

[45] Joshua's sister, Elizabeth and her husband, James Rogers.

[46] Easter Rebecca Winters, Joshua's sister.

[47] He possibly meant Captain Flack.

[48] Richard Ball, a private in Co. G. He and his parents, born in England, lived in Benwood, Marshall County in 1860. Census.

[49] Unknown. May be Curry.

we was revewed today by Generel Stergers[50] on the hill between Fort Work and Fort Warren. July the 22 Thursday. no noos today. the 23. cloudy. genl drill us today. no noos to day. the 24. beautiful day. we got marching orders to day. i got mi lettres to be in the [?]. it is purty tite today. sum fiting. the 25. nice day. we left Camp Pope friday the 25 in the morning. got on the cars. got to Warrenton four in the eaving. warm day. the 26. we moved our camp one mile from Warrenton. it is a beautiful day but warm. no noos today. 28. vary warm. i am on quarter gard to day. thair is no noos to day. the 29. it is warm to day. no noos. the 30. it is warm. i took a walk to day out after bearies. it is litning vary mutch to night. the 31. it is a dark morning. no noos to day.

August the first. beautiful morning. Canons a firen. four shots then one every hour through the day. the 2. nice day. got marching orders. left Warrenton 3 in the eaving. marcht to the Sulfer Springs. got hear at sun down. the 3. i am on gard this eaving. it is a raining. the 4. we was on a grand revew, revued by Generel Mac Dowl[51]. i washd mi cloths this eaving. i hav a vary bad cold. the 5. vary warm. we left Sulfer Springs this morning at six oclock, marcht 9 mils, got to the Rapadan river. the boys is all in a sirmon. the 6. we left this morning at six. nice day to march. we marcht till 12 to day. camp in 2 mils of Culpeper. the seventh. beautiful day. i had potato and roustin ears for supper. no noos today. the 18. warm day. no noos to day. at four in the eaving we got marching orders. we went to Culpeper, stopt till dark, then went 2 mils further. camp in the woods all night. the 9. all quiet. the trupes passing here all night and still a going. at five in the eaving we moved, found the miskiting[52] over. we went to the frunt. i was on pickit. canonaiding vary near. the 10. we swerved back vary early expecting an attack but none today. the 11. wet day. a flag of truce today. thay are bearying the dead. no firing today. the 12. the rebels has left, our men after them.[53] it is vary wet this eaving. we are still in the same place. the

---

[50] Unknown. Possibly Gen. Samuel Davis Sturgis?

[51] General Irvin McDowell, twice defeated at Bull Run. He was in the Shenadoah at this time, commanding the Third Corps. Strother, 65.

[52] Joshua wrote of musketing and cannonading to refer to the firing of muskets and cannons.

[53] This battle, just south of Culpepper, described in more detail in the letter below, was known as Cedar Mountain, Slaughter Mountain, or Cedar Run, started on Aug

13. nice morning. the 14. beautiful day. the 15. wet morning. we hav got marching orders. we marcht 6 mils, camp in a meader, grass waist high. the 16. no noos. Sunday the 17. warm. no noos. got orders to move. we left at midnight. went three mils. stopt till day light.

[13]

Miss Anna M Winters
elm grove Ohio
County va

[Postmarked] Washington, D. C. Aug 15 1862

Camp Six Mils South of Culpepper
Wenzayday August the 13

Dear sister,

it is with plazure that i take my pen in hand this morning to let you no that i am well at presant and i hope these few lins will find you all the same.

Well Mary i received your letter amunday. it was dated august the first. i was glad to hear from you but sorry to hear that Kezia[54] was sick. i hope she is well by this time. i rote to you last week. well i recon you hav heard of the battelling out hear on the ninth. we wasint in the fight. we was six mils back. we got up at dark; the fight was over all but the canons. thay cep ashooting till midnight. our brigaid went in front on pickit. the first thing we node we was in one hundred yards of the rebell battery in the woods. we was under the hill. i was on gard in front of our regement. the canons opend, we laid close to the ground. the balls went over us. i could see the flash of the guns. nun of us was hurt. sum of thair collum laid to our right. we could see them, hear them, and thout it was our min. we fell back before day light. our regement got off safe. one man was

9 and continued with skirmishes through Aug 10, Sunday. Total Federal casualities were 2381 out of 8000 troops, Confederates 1341 out of 16800, so there were a lot of dead to bury.

[54] Mary and Kezia are older sisters of Joshua.

wounded. the 1 Indiana lost sum. Generl Carl[55] stood gard all night. he says thay will never git him in such a nother place without he nose sumthing about it. a sunday the Crinishers[56] were firen all day. a munday a flag of truce went out to get the dead. thair was a ofell site on both sides. thay hav left now, our min after them. i don't no when we will move. i saw Charley Bary and Will Dougherty.[57] Charley is the same old boy. thair is anofell force hear. Well Mary, i will close mi letter. i must rite home. i will rite to you soon again. you must rite soon. tell me how Kezia is. i hope you all are in as good of helth as i am. no more at presant but still remain your kind brother,

Joshua Winters
to Mary Winters

rite soon. direct your letter to Culpepper. Good by.

DIARY. August the 18 1862. on our march. we got to the Rapahanac river about 10 at night, crost and campt. the 19. the rebels in sight. sum shelling. our begaid fell back a piece. the 20. i am on gard today. it is raining. sum shelling today. the shells hit our camp. the 21. we moved our camp into the woods. raining today vary hard. cananaidin all along the lins this morning. today, the 23, started to march. went six mils, stopt for the night. it is a raining. the canons is still a firing.[58] the 24. got up this morning at three. got ready to start. went in 3 mils of Sulfer Springs then stopt for the night. the 25. 2 oclock started again. crost the fields on the next road. staid thair all night. the 26. marched backwards and forards along the lins all day. the 27. started at 2 in the eaving, went till one at night then

---

[55] General Samuel S. Carroll.

[56] Joshua had trouble spelling "skirmishers".

[57] Charles Berry, age 22, was living as a hired helper in the home of Albert and Mary Davis in 1860. Albert was Joshua's uncle. William H. Dougherty, age 17, was living with William Dougherty, age 84, born in Ireland, Nancy 35, Catherine 32, Lavinia 29, and Martha 16, in Sand Hill in 1860. The Dougherty's have close connections with the Winters'. Mary (Winters) Daugherty was Joshua's aunt, but William does not belong to her family. He was probably her nephew, based on 1850 census listing.

[58] Skirmishing was recorded for the Rappahannock area on Aug 20, 21, and 23. Long, 253,254.

rest till morning. the 28.march all day till 12 at night.had a fight at the gap in the eaving. fell back.the 29.fiting on our left. stop at Manassus Junction for diner then went on up to the battell field. the 30 [August 1862] fiting at Bull's Run. our begaid in the fight today. we had to fall back. the 31. all got together at Sentervill, staid thair till after diner then started back. the rebels in frunt of us, in fields along the rode. i was on pickit at night.[59]

September the first. march to Fairfax Station. stop hear. vary hard rain this eaving. call up at midnight. laid in the woods all night. the 2. started at 5 in the eaving, marcht till ten at night then stopt till morning. the 3. started, got to Elexandria in the eaving. warm day, hard marching. the 4. warm. left Elexandria at 4 in the eaving, march till dark. the 7. started vary early, marcht through George Town. stopt for the night at 2 in the eaving. vary warm day. dusty. this is Sunday.

[14] [Addressed to:] Miss Anne M. Winters, Elm Grove, Ohio County, Va. [Postmarked] ______ling, VA. Sep 8

September the 4 1862

Dear Sister Anne,

i now take mi pen in hand once more to let you no that i am well and i hope you all are the same. this is the first chance that i have had to rite to you. i recon you have been uneasy a bout me. we are at Elexandria now.we got hear last eaving. we was in the fight at Fair Gap. our Orderly Surgent got shot thair in the hand. we was at Masses Junction.we lost five or six min thair out of our Co. our Capton and Lutenant is sick.the Kirnel is not expected to liv. the Mager is promoted. he leavs tomorrow. Thair is but one Capton in our regement that is fit for deauty. the rest is sick. we have had sum hard fiting out hear since i rote to you. our regement is small now, a grate menne sick. John aint vary well today. Jake is in the host pittell. Sam is grumblin. it is gitting

---

[59] Apparently Joshua's Company was just on the edge of the Second Battle of Bull Run, or Manassas, which was fought on August 29 and 30. Lee's forces were victorious but failed to route the Federal Army under General Pope. The latter fell back to Centerville where they were joined by additional forces but continued to withdraw toward Fairfax and Washington. The encounter at "Fair Gap," which Joshua's unit engaged in, would have been the Battle of Thoroughfare Gap, August 28. Long, 258.

late. i cant rite mutch this time. i will send this letter with Mager Devall in the morning. we are gitting along vary well now. I hurd that Isaac and Lonzo had inlisted. I wish you wood tell me what regement thay are goin in.

i must bring mi letter to a close. no more at presant but still remain your brother Joshua Winters
to Anne M. Winters.

rite soon. giv mi lov to all. i am in good helth and i hope you ar all the same. excuse this short letter. i will rite as soon as i can. good by again.

DIARY. September the 9. we left George Town at 9 oclock at night. marcht through Washington to Elexandria. campt beside Fort Elsworth. got thair at daylight. good deal of stragling. the 12. we left Fort Elsworth 3 in the eaving. marcht to Arlington Hts. stop for the night. the 13. went in to camp today. the 19. we was on a grand revew today. revewd by Generel Whipper.[60]

[15] [From Joshua's mother, Eliza Davis Winters, after she knew Joshua was not killed in the Second Battle of Bull Run.]

Sand Hill September the 20 1862

My dear darling son,

i take my pen in hand to let you know that the fue lins we got from you dated Sept 4 found us all well and thankful that you have been spaird thrugh all the dangers of hard fiting. we heard that the First Virginia at the Manases Junction was all kild or taken prisnors but two offesers, and oh, to think you was one of that number. how i wish i was on the battelfield that i mite hunt for you and find you alive and bring you home, but oh, how glad we all was when Kezia sent us word that you was alive and well. if you get sick or wonded let us no and Pap or i will cum bring you home.

i dont now what Peerpont[61] ment when he sent speakers to tell the peapel that they was a goin to draft. if it hadent a bin for

---

[60] General William D. Whipple.

[61] Francis H. Pierpont, provisional Governor of Western Virginia, headquartered in Wheeling.

the draft Isaac nor Jim[62] woodent a went but so it is and i cant help it. i wish that all of the drunken offecrs and all the liing speakers was out hear on Sand Hill in a sheep pen and all of the Sand Hill mothers was at the door with a iron poker a peace. i bet we wood keep them in till the war was over.

Lissa[63] and her littel babe is moved home till Jim cums back. she has gon to town to stay till thare rigement gos away. well Joshua, i want to now if you have enny meeting of enny sort sence battell died[64] and how you are a gittin along. i wish this war was over and you was all home once more. i hope it wont bee long and it is my dayly prare that you will all cum home safe. well i must bring my letter to a close for i am afraid you cant reade it. write as soon as you can and as often as you can. no more. i remane your loving mother till death.

Eliza Winters to her son Joshua Winters

[16] [from Anne to Joshua]

Saturday night
September 20 1862

Dear Brother,

once more in health i take up my pen to inform you that we are all Well at present and i hope that these few lines that i am am about to rite may find you enjoying good Health. Well Josse, Easter got a letter from you last night dated Sunday the 14 and you better believe we was glad to hear from you. We did not no but what you was killed. Well Josse, Sand Hill is a lonesom place now since Captain Flack's[65] Company left here. there has been nothing going on this week but this night a week ago i was at a sining at the school

---

[62] James Rogers, who married Joshua's sister, Elizabeth. He enlisted in the 15th WVA Regiment, Co. I., along with Isaac and Alonzo. Both Isaac and Jim were married when they enlisted.

[63] Elizabeth (Winters) Rogers, Joshua's sister. Her baby's name was McClellan Rogers.

[64] The penmanship is very legible and this is what it says. We do not know what it means.

[65] Capt. David H. Flack, who lived in Sand Hill District near the Winters family, seemed to be instrumental in organizing Company I of the Fifteenth Western Virginia Infantry Volunteers. He mustered in at the same time the company formed, but was discharged April 1, 1863. Census and Adj. Gen. Rep.

hous. there was an affoul site of soilders. it was made for the soilders. they came out on Thursday evening. there was a sining at the School House but they did not get out in time. they started from Camp Willey at half after six in the evening and got home about ten oclock but the sining was out before they got here. that was last Thursday night a week, then a Friday there was a party at Abner Kimmins,[66] a Saturday thair sining so it keep them bussy. a Sunday ten of them went to Haney Town[67] to preaching. A Monday morning they started for Camp Wiley in good heart. So this is Saturday night again and it is very lonesom here. there was some of the boys came home this evening. then a few minutes after they got their furlough Captain Flack's Company was ordered to rais their tents. they are to be back at Camp tomorrow evening at 5:00. They are expecting to start tomorrow evening. You don't believe how lonesom we are. We just have one man left, that is Cousin John Dougherty[68] and we can't part with him. Tell Sam his mother wants him to rite her. When you rite tell me what has come of John and Jake and where they are at. i heard that they have had another dreadfull battle. oh when will men quit fighting. oh this dreadfull war. Wont you be glad when this war is over and settled.

Well Josse, us children has a grate time a helping Pap. Nancy and me went over to Nancy Dougherty's after a couple of calves. i chopped wood yesterday till i had a blister on my hand.

Dear brother, i laid your letter by last night. i will finish it this Sabbath Morning. it has just struck six oclock and i am done milking. we milk our nine cows. i have not eat my breakfast yet. Isaac come home last night. he is in for Corporal of the guards. he makes a fine looking officer. they expect to leave Camp for Clarksburgh a Tuesday. i expect the next thing we hear you will be in for Major or some other office. Do try and get a furlough this fall

---

[66] Abner Kimmins, age 33, Elizabeth, 26, Ellen, 6, and Josephine, 3, lived next door to the John Winters family in 1860. Census.

[67] Haneytown is now called Dallas, a small town in the northeast corner of Marshall County, three or four miles from where Joshua's family lived.

[68] Living near the Winters farm in 1860 was John Winters' sister, Mary, age 44, husband Robert Daugherty, 52, with many children including James W., 15, John W. Daugherty, 14, Robert H., 11, Daniel W., 10, Nancy E., 8, and several younger. Census.

and come home. we have got plenty of apples and peaches and plums. Lib has come home to live once more. Macca is a great big boy now. he can stand alone, almost. he is a great pet. Juila is a great big mare, big enough to ride if she was broke. i wish you wood come home and brake her so i could ride her. she is quiet. she will come up to me in the field. You said in your other letter to me you wanted to no what regiment the boys was in. They are in the fifteenth Virginia Regiment.

Well Josse, Mother and Pap sends their love to you. give love to all the boys but keep some for yourself and don't forget to rite. i hear that somebody up on the hill gets a letter now and then. i gess the rest of her family thinks you and her will be married as soon as you come back.[69] i recon so. Well i think i have done fine for this. i rite as this come to hand. i dont no wither you can read this or not. Well there is preaching this evening at Sand Hill; Mr. Larkin, a new preacher. i wish you was hear to go with me this evening. rite to me. Easter will rite in a couple of days. after this short letter i must rite a few lines to Lol. Remember me my brother dear though we are many miles apart, alas for thee and me. rite soon, rite soon, and dont forget your loving sister.

To Joshua Winters

Anne Maria Winters

DIARY. Sept the 20. i went over to Washington this eaving, and on apast. the 21. i am on quarter gard today. beautiful day. the 22. we was on a revew today - Gererel Whipper. Cavery maid sum charges. the 26. i was over to the 9 Va today. seen all the boys. i hav a headack. i am on the sick list today. Satterday the 29 of September. we got paid today.

---

[69] Beulah Jane Blake, whom Joshua eventually married, lived on "Number Two Ridge" which would surely be considered "on the hill". Joshua himself never mentions Beulah in any of his letters.

[17] October 1862 [No day]

Dear sister,

it is with plazure that i take mi pen in hand to let you no that i am well at presant and hope that these fue lins will find you all in good helth. well Anne i recived your letter last night and i was glad to hear from you and to hear that you was all well. well we ar still at Arlington Hts. this is a vary good place. we haint got paid yet nor we wont till next munth. it is a gittin right cold hear at night. thair is no sine of us a leaving yet. thair was a potition got up and we all sined and sent it to Peerpont to call us to Wheeling or sum place close thair till we wood all git home and get the regement filld up. we haint hurd from him yet what he will do.

thair is no noos hear to rite about. i hav bin looking for Charley Bary and Will Daugherty in today. thay ar campt 3 mils from hear. the boys is all well but Jake and Jim Simpson. thay aint vary well. you said it is lonesom on Sand Hill now and i expect it is. i dont see why you was so uneasy about me till you got the letter i rote to Easter for i rote two or three to you befor i rote that one after we cum from Bull's Run. you wanted to no what has becom of John and Jake. thay rote you a letter the outher day. it is vary warm today. we hav no pickit to stand hear nor not mutch drill. our Capton is still sick. i recon the boys is left Wheeling by this time. if we git to go back to Western Virginia we will be apt to see them. i hope we will go.

well i recon thair wont be vary menne appel pairings[70] this fall. i wish Pap wood quit plowing for if he dont his lag will git worse. i hope we will all get home this fall for i dont see how you all will git a long this winter for wood and with the feeding. it may be over before long but it is hard to tell. i recon the boys had a big time before thay left. i think i will bee home before Chrismass. well in time to hav a slay ride. well i cant think of enne thing more to rite. tell Mother i will anser her letter this week. i hope these fue lins will find you all well and if you get lonesom keep in good hart. thay say every thing is for the better. i will bring mi letter to a close so no more but still remain your brother till death.

Miss Anne Winters — Joshua Winters

---

[70] A social/work event. Apples were peeled and apple sauce and/or apple butter was made. Some pared apples may also have been placed on screens to dry.

good by but i hope not for ever.
remember me when this you see though menne mils apart.

Giv mi luv to Pap and Mother and all the children and keep a shear for yourself.

[Apparently Joshua was home during October and November 1862. He didn't write in his diary during that period.]

[18] November the 30 [1862]

Dear sister,

once more i take mi pen in hand to let you no that i have a rived at Cumberlent safe. we had a vary cold ride of it. the cars stopt at Pigemont, [Piedmont] got watter, and so thay woodant hafto stop at New Crick but thair was a bout one hundred of us jump off and staid till yesterday eaving. got on the pasinger car. Thay tride to make us pay our way on the cars but thay coodant cumit.[71]

i found the boys all well but Hudson.[72] he is vary sick. sum of them is vary tired of soulderen areddy. the boys is all gone to church. i thout i wood stay at home and rite. i am going this eaving.

we haint got fixt up yet. if the boys beehave we will stay hear this winter and if not we will go. i haint bin throu this place yet. it looks like a vary purty place, and nuthin is to hinder you from cuming out this winter. well i didant git out again. thair was no locket at Kezias. Lol is cumin up to see us and we will both git them taken in one and send it to you. the first time enne of you is in town git yours takin on paper and send it to me.

we had a vary good supper in Wheeling. well Anne, i cant rite mutch this time. i will try and rite more the next time. direct your letters to Cumberlent.

no more but remain your brother. giv mi lov to all.

to Anna M. Winters Joshua Winters

---

[71] "Thay" did not succeed in making the soldiers pay for their passage on the railroad. Those jumping off the cars at New Creek wanted to do so because the Company I of the Fifteenth Regiment was stationed there and they wanted to visit their relatives and friends.

[72] John Hudson Davis, son of Hanson, and Joshua's first cousin, was in the 15th WV, I Co. He later married Joshua's sister, Susan Nancy Winters. He was sick during most of his tour of duty and was discharged for disability on 26 Feb 1863. Archives.

[19] [From Anne to Joshua]

Sand Hill, Thursday
the 11th [Dec 1862]

Dear brother,

it is with pleasure that i take up my pen to inform you that i received your letter and was glad to hear from you. We are all well at present and hope that these few lines may find you well and in good heart. Well Josse, i did not think when you started that morning that you would not get back. Aunt Mary[73] had her wood chopping last Friday. She had no quilting. When you and Jake had to go i heard about the party you had in Wheeling and heard that you staid with Mag Roseberry, and the word came pretty strait for Emily Roseberry told it all over Sand Hill.[74] She was afraid we would not hear it. Well Josse, it is so lonsom I don't know what to do, but i hope the war will soon be over and you will all get home safe once more. Aunt Polly Daugherty is going to have a wood chopping and sewing this week or next. i expect it will be a whopper. Well Josse, Lib is just reading over some of your letters when you was in Fredericksburg. i had thought of lots of things today i allowed to ask you but i forgot it. Well you said you stopped at New Creek and seen all the boys and i suppose they was glad to see you once more. you said Alonzo was going to place you near and both of you was going to get your likeness taken in a locket and send it to me. i hope you will not forget it but i expect to look for it all winter and then not see it, but i hope my looking will not be in vain. i want them taken with as much of your uniform as well as your gun and all your buttons. But i am afraid you will forget it. well there has been no party since you left. i have never been away from home since you left. i got a letter from Lol and one from Jimmy Dougherty[75] the same day i got yours. i would of answered it if i could of got it sent. Lib says she misses you very much at night about nursing Macca. he cant walk yet. Well there has been no preaching since

---

[73] Probably Hanson Davis' wife Mary.

[74] 1860 Marshall County census, Dallas P. O., William and Eliza Roseberry with Emily, age 19, Margaret E. 16, and John, 15, lived very near the Winters farm. (Margaret married Thomas Jefferson Winters, son of James. He was Joshua's first cousin.)

[75] Another of the children of Robert and Mary "Polly" Daugherty, hence Joshua's cousin.

you went away. there was preaching at Coffee Town[76] last Sunday night. Abner Porter[77] came home with Martha. they had a grate time coming home as it was raining very hard. i heard the other day that Charlie Berry had to stand guard forty days and forty nights for coming home that time but i dont believe it. Well Josse, Tofil is dead at last. she was very sick two or three days before she died. Well i must bring my letter to a close by asking you to rite soon. Lib sends her love to you and says she will rite soon. the rest of the children sends there love and also Pap and Mother sends there love to you. i want you to rite soon as you get this. excuse me for not riting more as i thought this was enough for this time. i still remain your sister.

Anna Maria Winters

to Joshua Winters. rite soon. give my love to Jake.

[20] [This letter is folded diagonally, and scorched in the folds.]

Munday morning
December 15 1862

Dear sister,

it is with plazure that i now embrace this opportunity of riting you a few lins to let you no that i am well at presant and i hope these few lins will find you all well.

Anne i received your letter yesterday and was glad to hear that you was all well. we ar at North Mountain. we left Cumberlent one week ago to day. this is a vary pretty country. when we have dress praid thair is about 25 girls coms to see it, sum vary pretty ones. i haint been on picket since we com hear. the boys all gits thair supper and breakfist on pickit. thair was one regement com hear on thirsday and one battery this morning. Thair was eight Co. of Cavary and one peace of artilry went out in a [Cout]. thair is sum talk of us

---

[76] Coffee Town was a community center located on Stone Church Road between Sand Hill and Elm Grove. It is remembered by older persons as a place where preaching, singing, spelling bees, community dinners and like events were held. In the early 1900's it was an active center but does not exist today.

[77] 1860 Marshall County census; Alexander Porter, age 42, wife Sarah, children including Abner, age 18. Martha is presumed to be Martha Daugherty, sister of Will. Martha was age 16 in 1860.

a goin back to Cumberlent a wenzday. the reazen we had to com hear was that the 126 Ohio was a fraid to com. thay had 900 min to and the workmin was a fraid to com with them to fixe the railrode. After we com Generl Keley[78] told them that a littel Virginia regement wasant a fraid to go without Catteridges. we had nun till we got here. Thay ar hear now and our boys has them pretty near sceared to death. i haint got a letter from enne of the 15 yet.[79]

it is vary pretty wether out hear. it is warm and we ar all well and waiting pashintley to hear how Burnside[80] is getting along at Fredericksburg. he has bin doin well the last fue days.

our Capton is not with us now. he is attending a Cort Marshall in Cumberlent and out first Lutenant is agoin to try to go home to day. his wife is sick. well it is diner time and the mail is goin to leav at one oclock. a boy that stays in our tent carys the mail now. all the boys is out in the Cunttery. they will be in after a while a bragin about a good diner thay had. i had a big pone last week.

well Anne when you rite tell me all the noos. Jim Simson has just com in and diner is reddy. the mail will soon go. rite and tell me when you [hear] from Will and John Dougherty. Giv mi lov to Pap and Mother and Easter, Nancy, and Alle and Lib. Kiss Mac[81] for me.

mi lov to you and all the friends. i will bring mi letter to a close by asking you to rite soon.

Joshua Winters to Anna M. Winters

When on some far and distant plain, turn hear your eyes and read the same, and call to mind a brother so true, Who never again may be with you. Good by, rite soon.

---

[78] General Benjamin F. Kelley had recruited the first regiment of loyal Union troops south of the Mason and Dixon line and is credited with saving West Virginia for the Union. He commanded in the Department of West Virginia and was fiercely proud of his West Virginians.

[79] Joshua's brothers Isaac and Alonzo enlisted in Co. I of the 15th West Virginia Regiment, which mustered in 11 Oct 1862.

[80] General Ambrose E. Burnside.

[81] Joshua's baby nephew.

1863

[21]

North Mountain
January the 1 1863

Dear sister Anna,

i now take the plazure of writing you a line or two to let you no that i am well at present and i hope these fue lins will find you all well. this is Newyears day. it is a vary beautifull day and we hav spent this day with more plazure than we did last Newyears at Romeny. yesterday thair was two big boxes com to our tent. it took six men to cary them and one big one com today. we had a oster[1] supper and every thing good for supper last night. we had turkey and pound cake and pies, appels, chicken, and ever thing that is good for diner and a nuff left for two days yet. then i recon when that runs out we will git more. o yess i forgot we had wine too but thair was no girls hear for to wate on the tabell.

Thair has been som talk of Stuards Cavery[2] a comin hear but i gess it is onely talk. thair aint mutch danger. last night after we all laid down the dutch Cavery[3] got drunk and fired a good menne volleys. we thout thay was a coming for surten. we got our things on and out before we node what was up. thay was put under gard. our colonel told us that we wood stay hear all winter. it is a vary good place to stay. i am still a cooking. we haint had enne cold wether yet. i receved your letter a Tuesday and i got Easters since i set down to anser yours. i beleve i told Mother in the letter i rote to hur about being up to see the boys at Christmas. John was well. Jake and Jim Simson went up thair to day. i will finish your letter when thay com back. i gess thay will com back tonight.

Well, Jacob[4] has com back. the boys is all well in Co. I. Thay got thair box last Satterday. i was at church last Sunday night at Hedgvill.[5] quarterly meeting commences thair Satterday. Tell Easter i will anser her letter soon. the boys in our tents is well

---

[1] Although it seems fresh oysters would be hard to acquire in those days and times, Joshua refers to them on several occasions.

[2] Jeb Stuart, Confederate General.

[3] "Dutch" would mean anyone with Germanic ancestry, such as Penna. "Dutch."

[4] Probably still Jacob Soles, whom Joshua usually calls Jake.

[5] Hedgesville.

and all in good hart. well Anne i cant think of enne thing more to rite at presant. when you rite tell me if Pap got a letter that i rote and if mother got one. Giv mi luv to all. write soon and tell me all the noos. no more but still remain your brother,

Joshua Winters

Miss Anne M Winters Good bye

when you write tell me if you want your letters drected to Elm Grove or to Fair Hill.

DIARY.

Joshua
Winters
Cumber land
Md
North Mountain
VA

Thur Jan 1 1863. we ar at North Mountain. beautifull day. not out of camp today. we had a good diner today. i got a letter from home today the boys is all in good hart. Friday 2. beautiful day. warm. no noos today. the boys is all a fixin thair tents. good diner today. Saturday 3, nice day. no noos today. Robert Dougherty and John Roseburry[6] came hear to stay all night. Sunday 4. nothing of importance today. it raind this eaving. Monday 5. beautifull day. the fifty forth left hear last night for Romeny. the boys has gone to

---

[6] Robert M. Daugherty, age 24, and John T. Roseberry, age 20, were mustered into Co. I of the Fifteenth on 11 Oct 1862. Powell, 239,240. They were stationed at Cherry Run at this time. John was listed as age 15 in the 1860 census.

church to Hedgvill. Tuesday 6. it rained today. nuthing of importance today. Wed. 7. Clear and cold. we had a argment from dark till 12 at night. no noos today. Thursday January 8. this is mi birth day.[7] it is snowing. Friday 9. Clear and cold. Sat. 10. it is snowing vary fast. cold. Isaac was hear a littell while today. Sun 11. Snoing and sleating to day. i was at church to night at Hedgvill. Mon 12. nice winter day. Jake and me went to Cherry Run and staid all night with Co I of 15 Va. Tues 13. nice day. i hav just returned from Cherry Run. the sno is goin fast. i got a letter to day. Wed 14. it is damp today. we hav been gittin out staves to fix our tent today. Thurs 15. cloudy. we raist our tent today on staves. Fri 16. damp this morning. cold and freezin this eaving. Sat 17. it is vary cold today. i went up to Cherry Run this eaving, staid all night. Frank[8] was thair. Sun 18. i hav just return from Cherry Run. it is a nice day. no noos today. Mon 19. it is a vary pleasant day. i got a letter today. we hurd today that our army had capterd.[9] Tues 20. nice day and no noos. it commenced to snow tonight. Wed 21. vary stormy, snowy and cold tonight. it is freezing. no noos today. Thurs 22. damp day. Fri 23. beautifull day. i was at George Town at Church today. Mon 26. no noos. Tues 27. William Shriner[10] got his discharge and went home today out of our tent. Jan 28. it is a vary disagreeable day. it is a snoing vary hard. i got a box from home today. Thurs 29. the sun is a shining. the sno is about 14 inches deep. Fri 30. we had a sham battle of snoballing this eaving. Sat 31. nuthing of importents today. i got a letter from home.

Sunday February 1 1863. nice day. Mon 2. the snow is goin off today. no noos. Tues 3. it is clear and cold. Wed 4. clear and cold. Thurs 5. it snode all day. we got paid today. i drawd 36 dollars. Fri 6. clear day. no noos. Sat 7. pleasant day no strange noos today. Sun 8. beautifull day. nothing strange. mon 9. clear. no strange noos. Tues 10. clear. i am on qurter gard today. Wed 11. i hav been helpin the lieutenant to fix his tent today. it snode this eaving. Thurs 12. no strange news today. it raind sum.

---

[7] Joshua was twenty.

[8] Unknown. Joshua had a cousin, James Franklin Winters, called Frank, who could have been visiting his brother and cousins Company I at Cherry Run.

[9] Joshua did not say what or who had been captured.

[10] William Shriner, Private, mustered in 11 Aug 1862. Atty. Gen. Rept.

[22] North Mountain
February the 12 1863

Dear Sister,

it is with pleazure that i seat mi self for the purpis of ansering your letter whitch i received the other day. i wood of ansered it yesterday but i was helpin the Lieutenant to fix his tent all day. Well Alle i am injoying good helth and i hope these fue lins whitch i am now a writing will find you all the same. i hurd from Cherry Run yesterday. Jake was up thair all night. thay ar all well. i am a goin up thair the last of this week to stay all night if nothing happens. Well Alle, thair aint enne strange news. Hear we hav vary good times. Hear thair is no drill. Hear we ar on gard about once every ten days. Well Alle i was glad to get your letter. i want you to rite as ofin as you can. has enne body rode Julie since i left. when you rite tell me about how you and Jimmie[11] is gittin along and all the news. Well Alle i believe i will hafto close. mi pen is so bad i cant rite.[12] giv mi lov to Pap and Mother and Lib and Anne and Easter and Nancy and keep sum for yourself. your loving brother,

Joshua Winters

to Alle E. Winters. tell Nancy i rote to her a Sunday and i will rite to her soon. i hant time to rite to her now and i have no noos to rite now. Alle, rite soon. Good by

DIARY. Friday February 13 1863. clear day and no noos today. Sat 14. beautifull day. i went to Cherry Run this eaving on the cars. Sun 15. warm day. i walked from Cherry Run to North Mountain today. Mon 16. the sun is a shining. it is a nice day. Tues 17. it snode vary hard all day. Wed 18. it has been a raining and a sleeting all day. no strange noos. Thur 19. clear, no noos. Fri 20 clear. the snow is most gone now. Sat 21. clear and cold. we had dress praid this eaving.

---

[11] James A. Dague, son of Daniel and Eliza (Luke) Dague, eventually married Alice (Alle) Winters. His brother, William Dague, married her sister, Easter Winters.

[12] It is interesting to speculate about his pen. This letter is clear and legible, with no evidence of a bad pen. Some letters and particularly diary entries are in pencil but most are in pen and ink. The fountain pen was invented in 1884 but steel pens were in use much earlier. He would have to dip the pen in ink and he seemed to have it with him every day. How did he carry ink in his knapsack without spilling it?

[23] North Mountain 1863
February the 22

Dear Sister,

it is with plazure that i enjoy these lazure moments in writing to you to let you no that i am injoying good helth and i hope this letter will find you all in the best of helth and in good spearts. well Anne, i receved your letter and was glad to hear from you. i was sum what supprised when i opend your letter and found it was from you for it has been so long since i hurd from you. Well Anne i shood of liked vary mutch to of been at the party that you had at Ants. i hope you all injoyed your selfs. well you said that thair wood bee a singing at Nance Doughterty's.[13] i hope you will have a good time and all of you get a beau a peace. Well Anne i was up at Cherry Run this night a week ago and all the boys was in tolarbell good helth and thay appear to bee gittin along vary well. i didant see Jimmy Rogers[14] but thay said he was better. we have a splendid time hear this winter besides what we had last winter. we have nuthing to do but go on gard once every two weeks or so but i hope next winter we can enjoy our selfs at home. when you write tell me if enne of Unkell Hansons[15] has been over yet or not. i hurd Albert[16] was goin to git miried. Well Anne i got a letter from Marthe[17] the other day. she appears vary mad because i left her pickture at home. she said that she hurd that i had said to tair it up or breke it and everything else but dont say enne thing about it to enne one nor to hur. i will sent hur a fue lins befor long and tell hur sumthing and if she calls for it give it to hur but dont say enne thing to hur nor enne body else.

Well the drums is a beating and i must go to role call. it is over now and i will finish it tomorrow for it is gittin late now.

Well Anne i now sit down to finish your letter. it commenced to snow last night. it is about a foot deep and it still a snowin. i had

---

[13] Probably the home of Joshua's friend, Will Daugherty, where Nancy, age 35 in 1860, was the oldest female, rather than at "Aunt Polly Daugherty's" where the daughter, Nancy, was only 8 in 1860.

[14] Joshua's brother-in-law.

[15] Hanson Davis, brother of Joshua's mother.

[16] Albert G. Davis, son of Hanson, married Lavisa (Burkham) Helfenbine on 31 March 1864.

[17] Probably Martha Daugherty.

alloud to go to George Town to Church today but it is to bad to go. i guess thay will draft before long. Well Anne thair is no strange news hear to tell you about. tell me all the news when you write.

This day one year ago we was at Paw Paw on Grnd Reveue. Generl Cander [Lander?][18] was thair. we fired slutes because it is Washington's birthday. i will close. give mi love to all and mi best respects to all the purty girls. write soon. no mor at presant but still remain your lovin brother

Joshua Winters.

to Sister Anne M. Winters. write soon. good by.

This letter will leave hear on Munday the 23. this is Sunday. i have told you all the news now and you can tell Alle and Nancy that i will write the middle of this week to them both.

DIARY. Sun Feb. 22. it snode last night and all day today. it is a foot deep. Mon 23. it is clear. the sun is a shining beautifull. Tues 24. clear and pleasant. Wed 25. clear and no noos. Thur 26. damp day. Fri 27. pleasant today. Sat 28. plesant day. the snow is most all gone.

Sunday March 1, 1863. plesant day. Mon 2. beautifull day. we had drill and dress praid today. Tues 3. it is a damp day. Wed 4. Clear. Thur 5. clear and cold. we had drill and dress praid. Harvey[19] was hear tonight. we got marching orders today. Fri 6. clear. we left North Mountain at three oclock in the eaving on the cars. staid in the cars all night. Sat 7. it raind all day. we arived at Grean Springs earley this morning. staid in the car till eaving then put up our tents. staid all night. Sun 8. we left Grean Springs 9 in the morning, past through Springfield, stopt at Chain Bridge for diner, got at Romney at dark and campt. it is araining vary hard to night. the rodes is vary muddy. our knapsacks at Grean Springs. Com 16 mils. Mon 9. clear. the wind is vary high. Tues 10. clear. we moved our camp today. Wed 11. it is vary windy. it snode sum this eaving. we had dress praid this eaving. no strange news.

---

[18] Unknown.

[19] William Harvey Winters, Joshua's first cousin.

[24] Romney Hampshire County
March the 11 1863

Dear Sister,

it is with plazure that i now set mi self to anser your letter that i receved yesterday and was glad to hear that you was all well. i hope that these fue lins will find you as thay leve me, that is in good helth.

Well Anne, we left North Mountain a Friday eaving on the cars, got to Grean Springs a Satterday morning, staid thair till Sunday then started for Romney. we go to this place at dark. the rodes was vary muddy and it was a raining but we got our knapsacks hauld. we ar campt in the same field we was in when we was hear before. it is a hard looking place. i was over in Romney yesterday and as i was goin down the windays like thay did when we was hear befor i seen mules and horses asticking thair heads out of the windays of sum of the best houses. thair is 3 regiments hear besides ours and sum artillary and cavery but two regiments is a goin to leve. Jim Marsh[20] is hear. i seen him yesterday. we aint got as nice a place as we had at North Mountain nor i expect we wont have till next winter.

i seen the boys at Cherry Run when we past. thay was all well but Isaac. he had the head ake. i hope we wont stay hear vary long. we ar 10 mils from the rail rode and we cant get the papers till thay ar old. we hated to com to this place. i am glad to hear that you had such a good time at the sining. i hurd all about it. i got five letters yesterday. thay told me who all got beaus. i wood like to be thair to go to sum of them. the boys round thair has a good time of it now.

Well Anne, you can tell Alice that i sent hur a presant today. it is at Kezia's. she can git it the first time enne of them is in town. Well Anne it is diner time and i will close sose the letter will go today. i will write more the next time. Rite soon and tell me every thing that you hear and see. Drect to Romney, Hampshire County Virginia. i cant rite this morning so no more at presant but remain your brother.

Joshua Winters to Anne M. Winters

Giv mi luve to all. rite soon. Good by.

[20] Unknown. No James among the Marshes known to the editor.

DIARY. Thur March 12. it is vary winday. it snode sum today. Fri 13. clear and vary winday. i was on pickit today on the South Branch at the farry one mile from Romney. Countersine shirt. Sat 14. clear and pleasant. we had regemental in spection and dress praid today. Sun 15. it thundered and litened, haild and sleeted today. we had dress praid. Mon 16. clear. the ground is white with snow. we moved our camp today three miles from Romney on the New Crick rode at the end of MacCanickvill Gap.[21] Tues. 17. beautifull day. i washed mi clothes tody. Wed 18. it raind this morning then cleard. cold. i was on pickit today three mils from camp on the Grean Spring rode. Countersine grenadear. Thur 19. clear and no news. Sun 22. it is a beautifull day. warm and plesant. Mon 23. pleasant day. i washed mi clothes today. Tues 24. i was on gard at the battery tonight. it rained all eaving and all night. the Countersine was Romney. Wed 25. pleasant day. we was haulling timber off of the hill to fix our tents. Thur 26. clear and winday. we raised our tent up on prickkits today. Fri 27. i am on gard today to the South Branch of the Potomac at Pancake Ford. thair was 150 men came out and staid all night 4 mil from camp. the countersine is beard. Sat 28. it sleeted and snode today. i got in to camp at 11 oclock. the rodes is vary muddy. Sun 29. clear and vary winday. no news.

[25]

Romney Hampshire County Va
Mechanicsburg Gap
March the 29 1863

Dear Sister Anne,

it is with plazure that i now enjoy these lazure moments in writing you a fue lins to let you no that i am well at presant and i hope that these fue lins will find you all enjoying the same blessen.

Well Anne, i receved your letter the uther day and was glad to hear that you was all well. the wether is vary changebell hear. it is vary winday today. i hurd yesterday that the fifteenth Virginia had left the railrode. i dont no wether it is so or not. we have got our tent raised up on puntions. we have got fixt up vary well hear but we have a heap of gard to do.

This time one year ago we was agoin down the valle between

---

[21] Mechanicsburg Gap

Strawsburg and Edinburgh. i was on pickit a Friday night. it raind vary hard in the morning. thair was 12 of us and about 8 oclock thair a hundred out of the fifty fourth come out and staid till morning. i guess thay was afraid of the bush whackers. thair was a mail boy killd the uther day by them but thay didant git the mail. we capterd some mail the uther day from the Secesh. we dont hear vary mutch news hear. we dont get the papers vary ofen hear. this is Sunday and i wood like vary well to bee at Sand Hill or Haneytown today but i think against this time next year it will bee over if thay have good luck. i dont think we will have as mutch marching to do as we have dun.

Well Anne, our tent smokes to bad to write and i cant think of enne thing to write eather. tell Nance that i will write to hur this week. tell me if Alle has got hur presant from Wheeling yet or not. Well you will hafto excuse me for not writing more this time. i will write more the next time so i give mi luve to all of you. no more at presant but remain your brother,

Joshua Winters
to Miss Anne M. Winters
Write soon as you can. Good by.

This is the way to drect your letters
Mr. Joshua Winters
Romney Hampshire County Virginia
in cair of Capton Melvin
Co. G First VA Reg Infantry

and for gracious sake dont put haste on the back of the letter nor soilder nor nuthing els. now dont forget.

DIARY. Monday March 30 1863. the sun is vary warm today and i am on pickit gard on the Grean Springs rode three mils from camp. the countersine was blunt. it commenced to snow 6 oclock tonight. Tues 31. it snode this morning. i cum off of gard this morning.

Wed April 1. clear and vary winday. i am on gard today three mils from camp on the Grean Springs rode. Thur 2. clear today but raining tonight. i com off of gard today. Fri 3. clear and plesant. nuthing strange today. we drilld in the manuell of arms in the street today. Sat 4. clear and plesant. i was on furtigue today on the mountain. Sun 5. the snow is about 10 inches deep. it was a vary cold night. Reinforcements com to us at 11 oclock. the rodes was vary muddy. Tues 7. Clear. we moved on through Deadmans Gap, 2 mi, then sheld them. 150 of us went a cross the river in to thair camp, crost in a skift. i got to camp at 12 oclock at night. the rest stopt. it was an ofell march.[22] Wed 8. clear today. the regement got in this morning at 8 oclock. com in wagons. all vary tiard. Thur 9. clear today. i commenced to cook today. we got orders tonight to have our knapsacks packed and to sleep on our arms. we got paid today for to munths. i got [??] dolars.

[26] [Postmarked] New Creek Station

Mechanicsburg Gap
Aprile the 9 1863

Dear Sister Anne,

I seat mi self for the purpis of ansering your letter whitch i received to day and was glad to hear from you and to hear that you and all ar in tolarble helth. A munday our wagon train went out after hay tords Morefield. our Cavary went out to gard them. four or five hundred Secesh Cavary made a dash on them and took five of our teams. Thair was som more of our Cavary went out. thay had a little fite. to of our Cavary got wounded. thay wounded 25 or 30 Secesh and took a Mager and a Lieutenant and four or five privats. Thair was a hundred of us out of our regement and a Company of the 54 Pennsylvania started out at three in the eaving, went twelve miles, got up thair at dark. The fite was over and our Cavary was acomin back.[23] we got up a hill and staid all night. we coodant hav enne fire and i thought we wood freeze to death. we sent back for reinforcements about midnight. thair was three hundred infantry and to peaces of artilary com up to us and in the morning we started on. we went through Greanland Gap on to the river. then we shelled them out of thair camp. then about one hundred and fifty of us went across the river in shifts and went up

---

[22] The only mention of a W. Va. fight in Long said, "fighting broke out ... at Goings' Ford, W. Va." on Monday April 6. We can't identify "Goings' Ford". This skirmish Joshua's group engaged in was at or near Greenland Gap, as indicated in the next letter.

[23] We cannot document this "fite". See note 22 on previous page.

the hollow into thair camp. thay cut the tung out of the wagon and left them. we burnt them, then crost the river back safe. it was three oclock in the eaving then and we was all pretty near give out and it was 23 mile back to Camp and we started hungree and tiard. we got in 12 mile of our camp against dark. then thay stopt the artillary. horses give out and all the min to but sum of us kep on to Camp. Thay got in about 8 in the morning. it wood of made enne body laff to of seen them a gitten out of the wagon and hobling in to thair tents. it is a vary pretty cuntree out thair but i will say no more about that. we got paid to day for to munts. it is a pretty day to day. i had no aggs a Easter Sunday. i was a wishing that i was at home to git sum aggs. well i hope these fue lins will find you as thay leve me, that is in good helth. well Anne, i cant think of mutch to write so i will close for the presant but still remain your brother

Joshua Winters

to Anna M. Winters. write soon. Goodby. Give mi love to all.

DIARY. Friday April 10 1863. Clear. we mustered today to see the strenth of our regement. Sat 11. clear and no news today. Sun 12. it raind today. Mon 13. clear and no news. Tues 14 clear and nuthing of importents. Wed 15. it has been araining all day. Thur 16. damp all day. nuthing of importance today. Fri 17. beautifull day. no news. Sat 18. clear. no news. i washed mi close today. Sun 19. vary warm today. it raind tonight. no news. Mon 20. it raind all day today. no news. Tues 21. clear all day.

[27]

Mechanicsburg Gap
Aprile 21 1863

Dear Sister,

it is with plazure that i now seat mi self for the purpis of ansering your kind letter whitch i received a fue minits ago. it was dated the 16th. i was glad to hear that you was all well. it has been wet wether hear for a fue days but it has cleared up again. i got a letter from Lonzo a fue days ago. he said that thay was all well. he stated in his letter that Flack has resined and gon home. thay will miss him for he was vary good to them. i wood like to no who thay will have for thair lieutenant. i think Bill Tomson[24] has had a good stay at home. our capton was hear to or three days last week but he is gon again. he will be back in a fue days to stay with us. Jake is well. he is at the river a feeding the fish. he is thair all the time and he never gits enne. he says he is a fattening them. you said in your letter you hurd Charleston was takin but it aint takin yet. thay will hafto do better than thay did the last time before thay can take that place. Thair is nuthing strange hear now. thair has been no scouting dun since i wrote to you before. when you write again tell me if Alle has got the pickture that i sent to her yet or not. we ar a gittin along hear fistrate. we have plenty of meat and potatos and soft bread to eat and the seventeen munts more will soon role around. then i will be clear of the servis. the time slips away vary fast to us out in the wooding cuntry or hilly cuntry; that is more like it.

i got a letter from Jim Rogers last week. he is a gittin along vary well. i gess he will go back to his Co. before long. i think the boys must have a vary good time at Cherry Run, thay have been thair so long. we have got our camp fixt up vary nice. i wood like to see twenty five or thirty of you Sand Hill girls a comin in our camp sum pretty eaving to spend a fue hours. Thair is but one sick man in our Co. he has got the ague. i was sorrow to hear of Joe Siberts[25] death.

well Anne i must go and git supper. i hope these fue lines will find you all as thay leve me; that is enjoying the best of helth. give mi love to Pap and Mother and all the rest and write as soon as convenant. tell me all that is goin on. i will close wishing you all the best luck this world can afford. Good by from your brother

Joshua Winters

to Anne M. Winters. give mi love to all the pretty girls. good by. rite soon.

DIARY. Wed April 22. the wether is fair. Thur 23. it is raining vary hard all day. Fri 24. it raind all day but cleard up this eaving. Sat 25. fair wether. we had orders to pack our knapsacks and bee ready to

---

[24] William Thompson, of Sand Hill, was in Co. I of the Fifteenth. Powell, 241.

[25] Joseph B. Sibert, age 23, was living with his mother Nancy, Fair Hill P.O., near the Marshes and Winters', in 1860 census. No military record found.

move in a moments warning. Sun 26. fair wether. excitement in camp. thair was 80 men went on a scout out of our regement. started at dark. Mon 27. fair wether. thair was 185 of us went on a scout to Greanland Gap.[26] we left Camp at one p.m. got to the Gap at daylight. went all night. vary hard march. 31 mils from hear to the Gap. Tues 28. it is damp this morning. we left the Gap this morning at 11, got to Berlington at 8 at night. the boys was all give out. we took all the wagons we cood find. com 22 mils today. Wed 29. fair wether. we left Berlington at 8 this morning. the wagons met us at the Junction. we all rode in to Camp. got in about 11. it was a vary hard march. we marcht 31 mils. Thur 30. sprinkling rain. we mustered for pay today.

Fri May 1. vary warm. Sat 2. vary warm and not mutch news. Sun 3. this is a beautifull day. we left Camp this eaving at 2 oclock for Greanland Gap. past through Berlington, campt five mils on the uther side at 8. Mon 4. vary warm today. sum rain. started 2 in the morning, went 12 mils then got our breckfist, then past through the Gap and Campt 4 in the eaving. we com 18 mils today. Tues 5. it raind all day hard. we had no tents. Wed 6. it still rains. thair was 8 of us went on a scout today. we went five mils from camp then staid all night. got plenty to eat. staid in a barn. Thur 7. raining still. we went to York on Thorn Run. got our diner then returnd to camp. got thair 4 in the eaving. went 10 mils today. had a good time. Fri 8. i am on pickit today in Greanland Gap. Sat 9. it is pleasant wether today. we moved our camp in to the Gap today on a steep hill. Sun 10. clear today. we got our mail. nuthing strange. Mon 11. clear and warm. no news. Tues 12. vary warm. i am on deuty today cutting timber for a block house. Wed 13. vary warm. nothing strange today. Thur 14. it raind today. Fri 15. vary warm. i am on pickit. left for camp 2 in the eaving. campt at dark. went 10 mils today. Sat 16. plesant day. on our march vary earlly. past through Rigvill. got our diner at Berlington. got to camp at five in the eaving. com 22 mils today. all the boys vary tiard. Sun 17. clear and plesant. we had inspection and dress perraid today. Mon 18. clear and winday.

---

[26] Greenland Gap is a natural water gap through New Creek Mountain, cut by the action of the North Fork of Patterson Creek through the Tuscarora sandstone. It was a natural passageway used heavily by both sides during the Civil War.

[28] [to Kezia Winters]

Wheeling, West VA May the 18th 1863

Dear Sister

i am a goin to send sum clothes to you for to keep till next winter for thay are to hevvy for to kairy this summer. Jake will send one over cote, one blankt, and one book. the rest belongs to me.

Joshua Winters
to Miss Kezia J. Winters

DIARY. Tues May 19. the wether is fair. no strange news today. Wed 20. this has been a vary warm day. i am on pickit gard on the Winchester Road. Thur 21. vary warm today. i com off of pickit today. we had battelling drill this eaving.

[29]

Mechancsburgh Gap
May the 21st 1863

Dear Sister,

i now seat mi self for the purpis of ansering your kind letter whitch i received to day and was glad to hear that you was all well. it is vary warm to day. i have just com off of pickit. it is rite cool hear at night. i wrot to Easter the first of this week. i believe i told her all the noos and i hardley no what to write as thair is nuthing strange hear. as this is the 21 i suppose thay ar a karying on strong at Haney Town. i suppose the militia will bee calld out before long for to stay awhile. the papers say that the south is a grate deal weeker than we thout thay was. the General that made the raid through Missippi says that he thinks that thay cant stand it mutch longer and the Richmond paper says that thay will soon hafto quit. perhaps it will be all over this fall or next spring. i suppose that you think that the war has just commenced becaus thair is a big excitement a bote it thair. i think thay get vary bad sceard before thay git hurt. Thair aint mutch danger of a vary big force ever gittin in to Wheeling. the rebels has lost a good General, that is Jackson. He is ded for sirtin this time.[27] the boys has all sent thair over cotes

[27] General "Stonewall" Jackson, Confederate, died on 10 May as a result of a wound received at Chancellorsville eight days earlier. He was shot by his own men who mistook him for a "Yankee."

home for it is too warm to kairy them if we should hafto march. me and Jake put ours in a box and directed it in Pap's name. he will find it at the Thornburgs store. tell him if he pleases to git it the first chance that he has when he is in town. it is paid fur. thay cost to mutch to through a way and thay ar to hevvy to kairy in the summer so we thout we wood send them.

well Anna you can tell Mother that i ansered hur last letter but i will write to hur and Lib the last of the week. i was a lookin for a letter from you all week, then i thout it kept you bizzy for to write to John and other places that i didant look for it rite away. it is vary fue letters that i git and vary fue i write and i dont intend to write as menne. i will write to you once a week or twice a week. it is ofell hot hear to day. i think we will have rain before long. Jake is well. i hope these fue lins will find you well. thay leve me in good helth. give mi love to all. i believe i will close for the presant but remain your brother.

Joshua

to Anna M. W. Write soon. Good by.

May the 22. i will put your letter in the mail this morning. i have just got a letter from Isaac. Thay ar all well. to Miss Annie M. Winters.

DIARY. Friday May 22. fair wether. Sat 23. it is vary warm today. i was on gard today. Sun 24. it is vary warm and a thundern. i have been sick all day. Mon 26. pleasant day. nuthing strange. Tues 26. fair wether. i was wagon gard today. we went 8 mils after hay. thair was a drill this eaving. Wed 27. pleasant day. we had drill this eaving. Thur 28. pleasant day. i was on furtigue[28] today a diggin rifell pits. thair was drill today. Fri 29. the wether is pleasant. we had dress praid today. Sat 30. vary warm today. thundern this eaving. sprinkling rain. Sun 31. plesant day. we had Co inspeckting this morning. this eaving we had regemential inspeckting.

Monday June 1. vary winday today. i am on pickit gard today on the Winchester rode. Tues 2. plesant wether. i com off of gard

---

[28] On fatigue a soldier was not in dress uniform. This would be suitable for digging "rifell" pits.

today. we had dress praid. Wed 3. raind today. we had dress praid. Thur 4. plesant wether. i am on pickit in Mechanicsburg Gap. Fri 5. it raind today. we had dress praid. Sat 6. it is a raining today. we got paid today for to munts. we had drill this morning and dress praid this eaving.

[30] Camp Near Romney
June the 6th 1863

Dear Sister Anne

it is with plazure that i now seat mi self this Satterday eaving for the purpis ov answering your kind and welcom letter whitch i receved a fue minits ago and was glad to hear that you was all injoying good helth.

Well Anne i wood like to no hoo told you that i was takin prisner and whair at if i was takin. i new nuthing of it. the Cavery has just fetcht in sum prisners. thay fetch in sum most every day. Well Anne we hurd that Vitchsburg was takin, then we hurd it wasant.[29] the latest that we hurd is that thay was in fifty feet of one anuther. i think that is vary close, rather to close to bee helthy if that is so. Thair is one thing that is so, that is thair has been sum hard fiting thair. i hope thay will have good luck and whip them.

Well Anne i have just com off of dress praid and i will finish your letter. we drill one hour every morning before breckfist. we ar on gard every third day. i guess thay ar about dun with the fort and the intrenchments, then our deuty wont bee so heavy. i got a letter from Isaac this week. thay was all well then. we got paid today for to munts. i wood like to bee at home to go to sum of the sinings and the qurterly meeting. we have preaching every Saboth in Camp. You said that you hurd that the stars and stripes was a floating over Richmond. i dont think thay ar. Well thair is nuthing strange hear a tall, nuthing new hear.

You spoke in your letter about shirts. i dont no what to say. we ar so far from the rail rode purhaps i wood never git them. you mite leve one at Kezia's and maby she will have a chance to send it out to me. when you write tell me hoo all gets beaus at the sinings. i hope these fue lins will find you as thay leve me, that is in good helth. well it is gittin dark and i cant think of enne thing to write

[29] Vicksburg was assaulted but not taken. The long siege was just beginning.

about. you must excuse this blotted letter this time. Jake is well. he sends his best respects to you. Give mi love to Pap and Mother, yourself and all the rest. i will close your letter asking you to write soon. From your brother

Joshua Winters. to Anna M. Winters.

Good by for the presant. i must go to the river now to wash mi self.

i never hurd what Alle thought of the pickture of our camp that i sent to hur. Give mi love to all the purty girls.

DIARY. Sun June 7. it is winday today. i am on gard on the Winchester rode. Mon 8. i com off of pickit today. it raind this eaving. Tues 9. plesant wether. we had battaling drill this eaving. Wed 10. i am on pickit today at Maccanicburg Gap. cloudy today. Thur 11. it raind today. we had battaling drill today. Fri 12. we had grand revew today. we sent our knapsacks and all of our baggage to New Crick today. Sat 13. vary warm. i am on battery gard. it is a litening tonight. Sun 14. warm today. we got marching orders for New Crick. we left Romney 4 in the eaving, marched till three at night, halted in a mile and 1/2 of New Crick. Mon 15. we marched in to New Crick this morning, Campt in Fort Bull. it is vary warm. grate excitement to day. Tues 16. it is warm today. i am on furtigue today. the 15 VA and the 2 MD com hear today. the excitement is still kep up. Wed 17. vary warm today. i was on furtigue today a digging rifle pits. Thur 18. warm in the fore part of the day but it is a raining vary hard this eaving. i am on qurter gard today. Fri 19. we left New Crick today for Cumberland on the cars. fixt the rode. got hear six in the eaving. it raind vary hard. our Co perrold the town all night. Sat 20. it raind all day. our Co perrold the town all day. went to camp this eaving one mile from camp in the woods. Sun 21. fair wether today. i was in town all day. we had dress praid today. no news.

[31]

Cumberland
June the 21st 1863

Dear Sister,

i take mi pen in hand this Sabbeth evening to let you no that i am well at presant and i hope these fue lins will find you all in good helth. i dont no what is the reason you dont write to me. it has ben sum time since i got a letter from home. we left Romney this day a week ago to com to New Creek. then we left thair a Friday and com hear. thay aint in twenty mils of this place now, and maybe a good peace further away before this time. Isaac and all the other boys was well when we left New Creek. i dont no when we will leve hear. it has been vary quiet hear for the last fue days. i dont no what is a goin on. the railrode is all tor up from hear to Martainsburg. the excitement is all over hear. i recon thair was a grate fus in Wheeling and in the cuntry. i hurd all the militia was out. Isaac told me that Pap was out to see them. i wish we had got to New Creek a littel sooner.[30] then i wood of got to see him. Co. I of the fifteenth sent all thair things in to Mar[y]land and i dont recon thay will ever git them. i wood like to write more but the mail is just goin. i must close for the present. write soon. mi love to all.

Joshua Winters

Anna Winters. Good by. i wood like to write more but i cant. the mail is just goin.

DIARY. Mon June 22. Clear today but raining tonight. i am on pickit tonight two mile from town in Marland on the Williamport rode. Tues 23. Clear today. we had dress peraid today. Wed 24. Clear wether. i washed mi clothes today. Thur 25. it raind today. i am on qurter gard today. Fri 26. it raind hard and studdy all day. no strange news today. Sat 27. Cloudy and raind some today. Sun 28. Cloudy. i am on pickit today at Talers Ford[31] two mile from Cumberland. Mon 29. Cloudy and sprinkling rain today. Tues 30. sum rain today. we mustered for pay. i am on gard today at the head qurters. Wed July 1. very warm today. we moved our camp to the ege of town. Thur 2. it raind this morning. vary warm this eaving. we had dress praid. Fri 3. it raind vary hard today. i am on gard. thundern and litning tonight. we got paid for two munts today. Sun 5. warm and sum rain. Co. inspecting and dress praid today.

---

[30] Apparently John Winters, alone or not, travelled from Wheeling to New Creek to visit with his sons, Isaac and Alonzo, but missed Joshua.

[31] Taylor's Ford.

[32] Cumberland Maryland
July the 5th 1863

Dear Sister,

it is with plazur that i seat mi self for the purpis of answering the fue lins that i received yesterday from you and hope these fue lins will find you as thay leve me, that is in good helth. when you write tell me how you spent the fourth. i spent mine vary well considern whair we ar at. Jake is well. when Tomsons[32] com after Jakes things let them have them. Thay wakened us up yesterday by firen 30 shots out of the artilary for the 4th. the sky rockets and bedlum was a goin on all night. i hurd thair was a picknick hear yesterday. our first lutenant has been under rest for to weeks. he got a dispatch that his child was ded and thay woodant give him a furlow and he went on his own hook. when he got off of the cars at Wheeling thay took him and sent him back. he didant get to see his child. i dont no what thay will do with him. i hope thay will let him clear. it is still a raining. well i will close for this time. write soon. tell me all the news. from your brother

Joshua Winters

Anna M. Winters. Good by

DIARY. Mon July 6. left Cumberland 10 oclock this morning. Took the Baltimore Pike. went 12 mils; campt at Flintstone. it is ofell hot. Second Merryland in the advance. Tues 7. we was on our march this morning. at 9 oclock thair was 4 regments past us. we marcht all night. campt three in the morning in one mile of Hancock. sum rain today. it raind vary hard in the morning; muddy. we cum 27 mils today. Wed 8. a raining vary hard this morning. we past through Hancock and campt one mile on the uther side. Thair is 6 regements to battery and the Renggold campt hear. the Cavery capterd 65 muls today. Thur 9. Cloudy today but no rain. we had regemental inspection. our division is campt hear composed of 6 regements to battery, battalling of Cavery. Fri 10. warm. we left Hancock this eaving at five oclock, marcht till two then campt. our begade com 10 mils. our Cavery had a scremish with the rebels. Sat 11. vary warm

[32] An extended family of Thompsons lived on Sand Hill in 1850 and 1860, headed by Rebecca, age 74 in 1860.

this eaving. at 6 we started on our march. went 4 mils and campt at Clear Springs. our Co. and one out of each regement went on pickit at Clear Springs in the morning. we pettrold the town. Sun 12. warm today. the rebels in site. we can hear cannading plain all day. we capterd sum prisners.[33] vary hard thunder storm this eaving. Mon 13. it raind vary hard all day. i am on duty today 5 mils from camp blockading the rode. Canans can be hurd vary plain. Tues 14. we got marchen orders this morning at 12 oclock. we loded and started. we campt in a mile of Williamsport in site of the 6 army corps. Generl Averl[34] reinforced Kelley. the rods is vary muddy. it raind vary hard this eaving. canonading can bee hurd plain. the rebels is acrost the river. Wed July 15. we left Williamsport this morning at 9 oclock. Came back within two mile of Clear Springs then took the uther rode. went to Cherry Run. all of Kelleys and Avrells forces is hear.

[33] [Still on the MD side of Potomac.] Cherry Run
July the 16 [1863]

Dear Sister Anne,

i seat mi self for the purpis of riting you a fue lins to let you no that i am well and i hope these fue lins will find you all well. i got your letter the uther day and was glad to hear from you. Well, the rebels is acrost the river. we was clost a nuf to hear them a fiting 4 days but nun of us was in a fite. we ar at Cherry Run. we com back from Williamsport to this place yesterday. when we past hear Co I of the 15teenth stopt hear and thay ar hear yet. Isaac and Lonzo is both well and all the rest of the boys. thay ar a gardin a boat hear and taken trupes across. i gess we will cross in to Virginia today. when we com out a past here i thout we wood have a fite but we didant. we was in site of thair pickits at Clear Springs. on the pike we hurd them a fitin for fore days. we thout we wood git in to it every day but we didant. i dont think we will see enne of them now for thay ar a goin as fast as thay can. our things is all in Cumberland yet and we all expect to go back thair soon.

---

[33] The aftermath of the Battle of Gettysburg (July 1-3), as Lee's troops were receding. Skirmishes were reported this day at Williamsport. Lee crossed into Virginia on the 13th. Long, 360-365.

[34] William Woods Averell, General, served in the Virginia Campaign and was transferred to the Department of West Virginia in 1863. Strother, 209.

well, the rebels got the worst wheeping thay ever got, not onely hear but every place thay ar. well i will close for the presant. i will write soon again. dont bee uneasy about us for we wont have enne fite. Give mi luv to all.

Good by from Joshua Winters to Anne Winters.

i will tell the boys to write you. Drect your letters to Cumberland. rite soon.

i seen Will Daugherty the uther day. He is well.

DIARY. Thur July 16 1863. Plesant today. Averls forces and the 14 and the 15 VA battery all crost the river today. Cananading can bee hurd plain this eaving.[35] Fri 17. raining studdy all day. we croast the Potomac 5 oclock this eaving. campt on the railrode at Cherry Run to night. Sat 18. plesant day. we left Cherry Run this morning at 6 oclock. Com 9 mils then campt till eaving. started again, went in two mils of Hedgvill, stopt for the night. Com 6 mile. Sun 19. plesant day. we can hear canading in the valley. the 2 begaid moved forard to Hedgvill this eaving. the rebels drove our Cavery in. our infantry drove them back. Sum shelling 2 mile from Hedgvill.[36] Mon 20. plesant day. all quiet till 6 oclock this eaving. the rebels drove our pickits in in our rear. we all fell in. our regement went out 2 mile then come back in. the hole command fell back to Cherry Run. Tues 22. We got hear at 2 oclock in the morning, waded the river. our Co is deploid, then we crost and deploid. went 1 mile, com back at dark, got our supper and laid at the river all night. Wed 22. plesant day. all quiet. our Cavery drove the rebel pickit in at Hedgvill. the militia is campt below us on the river today.

[34] Cherry Run

July the 22 [1863]

Dear Sister,

it is with plazer that i seat mi self for the purpis of writing you a fue lins to let you no that i am well at the presant time and i hope

---

[35] Long, 387. July 16; "In the aftermath of Gettysburg there was also skirmishing at Shanghai and Shepherdstown W. Va."

[36] July 18,19: There was skirmishing at and near Hedgesville and Martinsburg. Long, 388.

these fue lins will find you all injoying good helth. we havant been in enne fite yet. we was at North Mountain but we fell back to the place the other night. the rebel Cavary com in site yesterday eaving. our regement went across but thay was gon. we have one regement on the Virginia side. our Cavary has just com back. thay was five mile from hear. thay seen the pickits. our regement has waded the river three times this week. we ar now a laying along the river bank reddy to keep them from crossing the river if thay try it, but i think thay have more senses than to com hear to cross. i hurd that the Pennsylvania militia was a comin. we havant got the papers for a fue days so we dont no mutch about the Army that Mead[37] has nor whair he is but hurd that we have took 90 prisners in the late battels. that is doing vary well. i think thay will play out this fall, then we will all git home. the boys in the 15th is all well. i havant seen them today. i seen them yesterday. well one of the militia is hear now. he says thair is 30 thousand in six mile of us. we ar glad to see them a comin but i cant think that we will have enne fitin to do hear. well i looked for a letter to day but it didant com. i think i will git one tomorrow. this letter wont go today so i will finish it and send it tomorrow morning.

July the 23. well the mail has come and no letter for me. thair is no news this morning. mi love to you all. Good by. write soon. dont be uneasy for thair is no danger hear. i will write soon again. this morning we all moved back from the river into our old camp ground, put up our tents. the fuss is over. i recon thay have left thair. we will go to West Va before long. no more,

from Joshua Winters to Anna M. Winters.

write soon and tell me all the news.

DIARY. Thur July 23 1863. we moved our camp back from the river. clear. no news today. Fri 24. we left this morning, crost the river, went within a mile 1/2 of Hedgvill. all of Kelleys forces is hear. it was ofell hot today. i am on gard at the Col tent tonight.[38] Sat 15. warm this morning. all quiet. no noos today. this eaving it

---

[37] General George Gordon Meade, Commander of the Army of the Potomac at this time. He had just crossed the Potomac in pursuit of Lee on July 19. Long, 388.

[38] Joshua is guarding the Colonel's tent.

thunderd and litning. vary hard rain this eaving. Sun 26. clear today. our Co is on pickit gard today. i was 2 mile from camp on gard. Mon 27. raining today. i plaid the first game today that i ever plaid. Tues 28. clear and warm today. a vary hard thunder storm tonight. Wed 29. clear today. no news. Thur 30. thunderd all eaving vary hard. rain this eaving. no news. Fri 31. clear and vary warm. no news.

[35] July the 31th 1863
Campt near Hedgvill VA

Dear Sister,

once more i seat mi self for the purpis of writing you a fue lins to let you no that i am well and i hope these fue lins will find you all in good helth. Well, Anne i think that you have forgot to write to me enne more. i havant got a letter from you since the 12 of July. i think i have rote you 2 since then. i got a letter from Mary. Well we ar in a mile of Hedgvill. thair is not mutch noos hear. thair is no rebels enne ways close hear. the last we hurd of them thay was a goin tords Gordinsvill. thair is a good menne desurters a comin in. thair was a hole Co com in hear the uther day. thay say the suthern Confedersy is plaid out. every thing looks like as if it is so. i havant seen Isaac nor Lol for a week. we left them at Cherry Run. i believe thay ar thair yet. well i will finish your letter tonight. i think i will git one tonight for surtin.

DIARY. Saturday August 1 1863. We took up our line of march this morning at 9 oclock on the Shanghi rode. we marcht till 5 in the eaving. it was ofell hot. we com 15 mile today. Sun 2. on our march this morning at 6 oclock. Rough rode. we crost the Blumery Pike, past through [pue]town and campt all night. we com 16 mils today. vary hot. Mon 3. on our march this morning at 5 ½ oclock. went 2 miles and struck the Romney pike. Marcht to Big Capon, got thair at 11 oclock. Campt. vary hard thunder storm this eaving. we com 9 miles today. vary hot.

[36] Capen River August the 3 [1863]

Dear Sister,

i seat mi self for the purpis of writing you a fue lins to let you no that i am well and i hope that these fue lins will find you the

same. Well, Anne, i got your letter dated July the 27. i looked for it a good while before i got it. we left Hedgvill the next day so that is the reason that i coodant anser it. we have been a marchin for three days. we ar in 22 mile of Romney. we stopt today at diner time to rest till tomorrow, then we will start for Romney. it will take us three or 4 days to get thair. the wether is vary warm hear. All of Kelleys divisions is hear. Co I of the 15th is not with us. i gess thay ar at Cherry Run yet. thay was all well the last i hurd from them. well, i will write you when we get to camp again. it looks like it wood rain and i want to write to Kezia so i will close for this time.
From

Joshua Winters to Anne Winters.

Good by. rite soon.

DIARY. Tues Aug 4. On our march this morning at 8 oclock. Got to Blue's Gap at 11 oclock. Stopt thair for diner then came to French Town. Stopt for the night. raind hard this eaving. we com 17 miles today. Dubbell Crick this eaving. Wed 5. on our march this morning at 6½ oclock. Com through Romney, stopt at Mechanicksburg Gap for diner them marcht on to Burlington. got thair at 5 in the eaving and campt. we com 18 mils today. hot. we travelled fast. Thur 6. we moved our camp today, one mile to water. it raind sum today. no noos.

[37] Camp at Berlington
[about 6 or 7 Aug 1863]

Dear Sister,

i seat mi self this eaving for the purpis of writing you a fue lins to let you no that i am well and i hope these fue lins find you injoying good helth. Well Anne, i got your letter on the 31 and we started our march the 1 of August and i had no chance to send enne letter. this is the third that i have started to write to you and i think i will get this one off tomorrow. well we have been marchin for five days. we got hear yesterday and campt. we com about 100 miles. thay say we will stay hear for sum time. we ar in 15 mile of New Crick. this is a vary nice place. we had sum vary hot weather hear on our march. we stopt a half of a day at Big Capon to rest. i rote a letter then but i coodant get it off. i gess our knapsacks will be hear. Co I of the 15th wasant with us on the march. i gess thay ar at Cherry Run. i havant seen them for 2 weeks. i believe thair regement is in Romney. we didant stop thair when we com through. well i had corn for supper. we havant hurd enne news since we left Hedgvill. we dont no what is a going on. this is a vary pruty place to camp. thair is three regements hear. well, i will put the 2 peaces of letters that i started to write to you in this one. well i will finish your letter tomorrow.

August the 7

it is a nice cool morning. the boys is most all gone a fishin. Jake is well. when you write tell me all the news. tell me how you ar a gittin along with the harviss. i will write again the last of this week.

Giv mi luv to all from Joshua Winters
to Anna M. Winters Write soon. Good by.

DIARY. Fri Aug 7. Clear today and no noos. we ar campt at Berlington. Sat 8. clear and warm. our Co and Co C and a Co of the 29th started this morning to gard a train to Petersburg for Generl Avrell. we went 24 miles today then campt. Sun 9. hot. we started on this morning to go to Petersburg at 9½ oclock. Averells begaid is hear. we unloded and started back at 3½ oclock. Com back six miles then campt for the night. Mon 10. we started early this morning, stopt at Patterson Creek for diner, got to Berlington in the eaving. we rode all day. vary warm today. it thunderd sum this eaving. Tues 11. clear and vary warm. it thunderd this eaving. we had dress praid today. Wed 12. warm today. nuthing strange. we had dress praid and drill. litning this eaving.

[38] to Mary Winters

Burlington
Hampshire Co. Va.
August the 12, 1863

Dear Sister,

it is with plazer that i seat mi self for the purpis of writing you a fue lins to let you no that i am well and i hope these fue lins will find you all the same. Well Mary, i recon you have begun to think that i have forgot to write to you but i havant had much time to write this last munth or so and you being at home is the reson i didant write before now. i got a letter from Kib[39] a fue minits ago and i thout i wood rite to you sins i hadant ansered your last letter. this one will do both. tell Kib the stamp is all rite. i was glad to hear of Isaac a gittin home; if he only gits to stay a while.

the 8 of this munth our Co. started to gard a wagon train through from hear to Petersburg. it belongs to Generl Avels Cavary brigaid. it is 29 miles from hear. it took us three days. we had a vary good time. we got to ride back. thair was 120 wagons when we left Petersburg. the third Virginia was thair but i didant get to see Will or Charley. we got our knapsacks this week and i tell you we needed them for it was just five weeks since we had a change of clothes. we have travelled around a good deal since we left Cumberland and we have had sum vary hot wether to march in. i am a sittin on the hill in the woods above our camp a writing. this is a vary pretty place. i dont no how long we will stay hear. thair is talk of us a goin to Clarksburg. i dont no whether we will or not. i wood like to go thair vary well. Jake is well. he is a setting besides me a writing. i havant hurd enne war news for a fue days. i think the war will close inside of a year. i hope so enne how. well i will close for i have no news to rite. give mi lov to all. write soon as you can and tell me all the news that is a going on. no more at presant but remain your brother,

Joshua Winters

Good by to Miss Mary E. Winters

DIARY. Thur Aug 13. vary warm. i am on pickit gard today on the Petersburg rode 1½ miles from camp. Fri 14. vary warm in the forenoon. this eaving cloudy and a thundern but no rain. dress praid this eaving. Sat 15. we left Burlington this morning at 6 oclock. took the Petersburg rode. went 12 mile and stopt for diner at Williamsport then went 4 miles and campt at the Greanland junction. vary warm. Sun 16. we took up our line of march this morning at 6 for Petersburg. we arived hear at 1 oclock and campt. we com 19 miles. vary hot. vary hard rain this eaving. all of Avrells begaid is hear. Mon 17. clear and nuthing of importence today. Tues 18. warm today. i am on gard at the qurtermasters. Avrells Cavery begaid left hear tonight for Frankling. Wed 19. warm today and no noos. Thur

[39] We believe "Kib" is Joshua's oldest sister, Kezia.

20. vary warm today, our Co is on pickit on the Frankling rode. we had a vary good time. we cood hear cannadin this morning in the direction of Frankling.[40] Fri 21. warm. we com off of pickit today. Sat 22. vary warm. we had drill today. Jake went home today. Sun 23. plesant day. expect an attack tonight. Mon 24. cool and pleasant. our Co. is on pickit today. we had a good time. Tues 25. warm in the forepart of the day. vary hard rain and wind this eaving. Wed 26. Clear, plesant. we moved our camp today one mile and 1/2 from Petersburg. Thur 27. plesant day. no noos. Fro 28. warm today. our Co is on pickit. thair was 22 desurters com in the Frankling rode. Sat 29. plesant day. Sun 30. plesant day. Mon 31. plesant day. we musterd for pay today. Tues Sept 1. plesant day. our Co is on pickit today. Wed 2. plesant day and no noos.

[39] Petersburg, Va.
September the 2th 1863

Dear Sister,

it is with plazer that i seat mi self for the purpis of answering your welcom letter and to let you no that i am well and i hope these fue lins will find you all the same. well i wood of answered your letter yesterday but i was on pickit. our knapsacks got hear yesterday and we was glad to git them for it was vary cold hear at night without blankits. we would lay in our littel tents in the fore part of the night and in the after part we wood lay by the fires. i think i will have a good sleep to nite. this is the second time we have had our knapsacks since the 6 of July.

Sum thinks that we will go to Clarksburg, Va, before long but it is hard to tell. i was on pickit last week and thair was 22 rebels com in the rode that i was on and giv them selves up. Thay com from Lee's Army. the mountains is full of desurters and thay ar still a comin and i am glad to see them. it appears as though thay dont like the green fire that Gilmore[41] is a givin them at Charleston. thay ar a bout plaid out but all the souldiers thinks that the war will soon bee over and i hope it will. i suppose Pap and you girls had a

---

[40] August 19, 1863. "In West Virginia Averell's Federal raiders destroyed a saltpeter works near Franklin." Long, 399.

[41] General Quincy Adams Gilmore, was leading the bombardment on Fort Sumpter, Charleston SC, in late August 1863. Long, 398,399.

long and weery harvist of it. i ofen think that if i was onley close anuf to help you when i am a laying in camp a doin nuthing, but i think the time aint long now till we all bee at home again to help do the work.

i wont mail this letter till after the mail coms to night. i think i will git a letter from Isaac this eaving then i can tell you how Lonzo is. Jakes furlow was out yesterday. i look for him this week. Jake was vary sick when he left hear. Jim Simson is in the hospittell. Thair is nuthin goin on hear and we ar a gittin along first rate.

\ \ \ \ \ \ \

well Anne when you write tell me all the news for i havant got a letter or i havant got one from enne boddy only from you at home and Kib and Mary for 4 munts so you see i havant hurd enne news onley what you write. tell me all you can think of. well i will close for this time. giv mi love to Pap, Mother, and all the rest. no more but remain your brother.

Joshua Winters
to Anna M. Winters, Write soon
i recon it is lonesom since Lib has moved.
Good by. Write soon. J W

DIARY. Thur Sept 3 1863. it raind this eaving. Fri 4. clear. all quiet till eaving. the rebels attacked Stevens[42] at Moorefield. we fell back. our 4 Co dug intrenchments. the 29th tride to go through the Gap to Moorefield but fell back at dark. our Co and the 29th went back 12 mile to meet Stevens. Met him at 12. Sat 5. this morning at three oclock we started back to Petersburg, got hear before 8. lade in camp all day. both of our regements worked on the intrenchments. Stevens and 5 Co staid at the gun stock. all quiet today. Sun 6. Sum rain today. both of our regements digging on the intrenchments. the 54 com hear today. thay had a squrmish a comin. Sum Cavery com hear today. one Co of the 10th VA com hear today. Mon 7. clear today. our Co is on pickit today. nuthing strange.

---

[42] Unknown. Long, 404, reports "skirmishing at Moorefield and Petersburg Gap, W. Va."

[40] to Alla E. Winters September the 7th [1863]
Dear Sister,

it is with plazer that i now rite you these fue lines to let you no that i am well and hope thay will find you well and abell to do your share of the work. Well, Alle, i have just com off of pickit and eat mi diner and i thout if you woodant rite to me that i wood rite to you enne how. it is vary warm hear today and i am in the shade out from camp a riting. i wish i was at home to get sum appels or appel dumplings and sider. i want you to keep me sum appels for i am a comin home this winter i think. Well the last i hurd from Lonzo he was a good deal better and is a goin to try and git home. i hope he will git home a while. Alle, i want you to rite and tell me all the news. Tell Nancy that i will rite to hur the last of this week. Giv mi lov to Pap and Mother and all the rest. Well i will close.

From your brother Joshua Winters.

to Alle E. Winters rite soon. i wood rite more but mi pen is to bad. Good by

Tell Anne that i have just got hur letter and i will answer it the last of this week. Tell hur that i got hur uther letter and answerd it. No more

DIARY. Tues Sept 8. Cloudy today and no noos. Wed 9. clear and plesant. Thur 10. clear today. tonite at 9 oclock thair was 100 of us went on a scout. We waded the South Branch, crost the mountain, got to the North Branch at daylite. vary rough rode, steep and dark. Fri 11. went down the river and attacked the eneme. Drove them, took sum prisners, then took the mountain. got to camp at sundown. all vary tiard. rough rodes and hard marchin. the 11 of September the rebels supprised Stevens at Moorefield and took 150 of our regement.[43] Sat 12. Damp today. tonight at 9 oclock thair was 150 of us went scout, waded the river and traveld till 2 in the morning. stopt in the woods, side of the mountain. i am on pickit. dark. all tiard and sleepy.

Sun 13. at daylite the 54th deploid and we moved on along the mountain for 2 miles. then we went to the top of it. the rebels had left. we com back on the rode and got our breckfist. got in camp at

---

[43] Long, 408, says, "fighting flared ... at Moorefield W. Va."

2 oclock, all tiard and sleepy. we went 25 miles. Mon 14. plesant day and nuthing strange a goin on. Tues 15. clear and nuthing strange. Wed 16. Clear today. i am on gard at Col Mulligans[44] headqurters. Thur 17. Clear today and no noos. it commenced to rain tonight. Fri 18. it rained in the fore part of the day. then cleared. Cold. Sat 19. the wind is cold today. i am a working on the fort today. Sun 20. it is still cold. thair was preaching in camp today.

Mon Sept 21. Vary larg frost this morning. i went out 17 miles today on the Frankling Rode with the wagon train after hay. we started 6 in the morning, got back in the eaving. Tues 22. clear and nuthing of importence today. Wed 23. plesant days, cold nites. Thur 24. warm and plesant today. Fri 25. fair wether. i am on gard today at Col Mulligans head qurters. Sat 26. plesant day. i am on pickit over the river today. Mon 28. fair wether. i cut sum logs today for a house. Tues 29. warm today. i went with the train after hay today. we got it in 9 miles of Moorefield. We got paid today for to munts. Wed 30. plesant wether. we raised our house.

Thur Oct 1 1863. PLesant day. it commenced to rain at dark. Fri 2. it raind hard all day. clear and cold tonight. i am on gard in the fort at the qurtermaster. Sat 3. plesant day. Sun 4. clear and winday. Mon 5. clear and no noos. Tues 6 clear. i was out on a pass today. Wed 7. it raind today and tonight i am on pickit gard. Thur 8. clear today and nuthing strange. Sat 10. clear. Sun 11. beautifull day. thair was inspection this morning.

[41] [This poem, handwritten in Joshua's handwriting, was with his letters to sister Anne.]

The Song of the Shell
By G. Warren Newcomb

Sullen and strong and thick and tall,
Rises the bastions moated walls.
The glaces is smooth and the ditch is deep,
And the weary sentry may never sleep;
Over the parapet heavy and dum,
Peers the mouth of the barbette gun

---

[44] Col. James A, Mulligan, whose 23rd Illinois helped guard the B&O Railroad. He was mortally wounded at the second battle of Kernstown 24 July 1864.

While lightenings flash and tempests glow
From the gloomier casements down below.
Strong is the works and stout is the wall
But before my song thay must crumbell the fall
Crumbell away to a heap of stone
Mingled with the fragments of dead men's bones,
And red with the blood that flowed as thay fell,
Thair requiem sung by the howling shell.

Flaunting and boasting and brisk and gay,
The streets of the citty shines today,
Forts without and arms within
To think of surrender were deadly sin
For the foe far over the wave abide,
And no guns can reach o'er the flowing tide.
Thay cant through the air with a rush and a yell,
Comes the screech and the roar of the howling shell.

The popular city is all alive
With the bees that are living in the ancient hive;
And the market places are wasted and bare
And the smoke hangs thick in the poisoned air;
And ruins alone shall remain to tell
Where the hymn of destruction was sung by the shell.

Traitorous and bloodthirsty mad with wrath
Charleston stands in the nations path-
Stands and flaunts a bloody rag,
Insulting the stars on the dear old flag
But Sumpter is crumbelled and ground away,
And over the watter on furious wings
It sings of red-handed rebellion crushed down.
Short are its cadences, harsh its song,
It shrieks for the right and it crushes the wrong,
And never a blast shaking nethermost hell
Cried vengeance and wrath like the song of the shell.

Petersburg, Hardy County, West Va October 11th 1863
Joshua Winters Co G First West Va Volunteers
Infantry organized in Wheeling in the year of 1861

DIARY. Mon Oct 12, 1863. Clear today. i am on fitigue today a diging on the fort.[45] Tues 13. clear today and nuthing strange. Wed 14. clear and plesant. Thur 15. i am on pickit today. it rained all day and night. Fri 16. it is raining today. Sat 17. clear today. thair was a empty train hear today.Sun 18. clear today but rained tonight. Mon 19. plesant day. i am on fitigue at the fort. Tues 20. plesant day. i was out in the Cunttrey. Wed 21. plesant day and no news. Thur 22. plesant day. i was 7 miles from camp today. Fri 23. this is a damp day and nuthing new at Petersburg. Sat 24. it still rains.Sun 25.this is a plesant day. Mon 26. clear and no news.

[42] Petersburg Hardy County Va[46]
October the 26th 1863

Dear Sister,

it is with plazer that i seat mi self this eaving for the purpis of writing you a fue lins to let you no that i am well and i hope these fue lins will find you all well. i receved your letter yesterday and i was glad to hear from you. i looked for it one week before i got it. Well thair is nuthing new a goin on hear onely thair is still talk of us a leavin hear but we have hurd so mutch about leavin we wont believe it till we start we have nice log houses to stay in.i wish you cood see us at night when we git a big fire and our pipes lit and sit down. Well you spoke in your letter of Meade being whipt but he wasant. He fell back to Sentervill sose Lee wood follow him then Burnside got in his rear and tore up the rail rode that led to Linchburg. then Lee coodant get his supplies. It took him back faster than he com. when thay went through Warrenton thay said thay hadant got enne thing to eat for 24 ours. the paper says that the Army of the Potomac is a goin to take a new rout to Richmond i hope thay will and have good luck. Well Anne, i havant got a letter from the boys since i rote to you before. i dont no what is the reason thay

---

[45] Fort Mulligan was constructed by the Federal troops just west of Petersburg, and this was surely the fort Joshua and his unit were working on, since he mentioned being on guard at Colonel Mulligan's headquarters on September 16 and again on the 25th. This fort is located on State route 28 and is one of the best preserved Civil War forts in the state, with extensive breastworks and trenches still visible. Cohen, 24. It was donated for preservation in 1994.

[46] Petersburg is now in Grant County which was formed in 1866 and named for Ulysses S. Grant.

dont write. i wood like to hear from Lib and Jim.

Well i am glad to hear that thair is still sumthing a goin on at Sand Hill by the name of parteys and sinings but thair will bee sumthing in the name of a draft thair before long. it will make sum of them open thair eyes. Well Anne, you will hafto excuse me for this bad writing and blots for i am in a hurry and it is vary littell writing that i do. i have almost forgot. i havant rote a letter since June onely home and to Kib and Isaac. Jake is well. i will bring mi letter to a close. Giv mi lov to all. Write soon.

This is from your brother

Joshua Winters

to Miss Anne M. Winters. Good by.

DIARY. Tues Oct 27 1863. this has bin a plesant day. Wed 28. clear. i am on gard today on the Moorefield rode. Thur 29. clear today. i com off of gard today. it was ofell cold last night. the forg train went to Moorefield today. thair was upwards of 900 gards. Fri 30. clear today. Sat 31. it raind this morning. we musterd for pay today.

Sun Nov 1. clear. i am on pickit at Cunergam today. Mon 2. clear today. Tues 3. Cloudy and raining today. Wed 4. Clear today. i am on pickit on the Siniky[47] rode today. Thru 5. it is winday today. Fri 6. clear today but vary winday. i am on pickit on the Frankling rode. Sat 7. Clear today. all the men is on gard. i washed mi clothes today. Sun 8. araining and a sleeting today. we left Petersburg today at 11 oclock on the North Fork rode. the first Va and the 29th, one section of artilary, Co of Cavery, stopt for diner, campt at dark. com 15 miles, bad rodes. Mon 9. Snoing today. took up our line of march this morning at 7, went 9 miles, stopt for diner at Siniky Pass then marcht till dark. i am on pickit tonight. bad rodes. have com 8 miles since diner. Tues 10. on our march this morning at 7 oclock, stopt for diner. vary bad rodes. a mountain on each side of the rode. stopt at 4 in the eaving. vary good camp. cold today. Wed 11. took up our line of march this moring at 7, crost the mountain into Crab Bottom, stopt for diner then started again. met

[47] Cunningham Gap on Nov. 1, and Seneca Road today.

Avrell at Fleetown[48] then campt. plesant day. Campt in Crab Bottom.

Thur Nov 12. Beautifull day. on our march earley this morning, went 10 miles then took diner, then past 1 mile beond Frankling, then campt. Avrells begade in the advance. the rodes vary dusty. we have com 19 miles today. Fri 13. vary warm today. the rodes is vary dusty. on our march earley this morning. we com 10 miles and halted for diner, then marched in 10 miles of Petersburg and campt. we marched fast today. Sat 14. on our march this morning before daylite. arived in Camp at Petersburg at 11 oclock. all glad to get in camp. our hole march was 109 miles. Averls begade is hear. sum rain today. Sun 15. it raind today.

[43] Petersburg, West Va.
November the 15th 1863

Dear Sister,

it is with plazer that i seat mi self this Saboth eaving for the purpis of answern your letter whitch i received last eaving when i com home. we left hear this day a week ago and got back last eaving. we started up the North Fork of the Potomac. we marched to days up a hollow. you could see nuthin; a mountain on each side. we seen sum farms a bout as large as Bruce's.[49] we went through Siniky [Seneca] Pass. Thair was sum vary pretty scenery; rocks in all shapes and vary high mountains. when we got to the head of the Potomac we crost the mountain into Crab Bottom, went down in within 6 miles of Monteray. Thair we met Generl Averl. then we took anuther ride and went to Frankling and com down the pike to Camp after we crost the mountain into Crab Bottom. we got into a beautifull Cuntry from thair to camp. the rode was vary dusty from Frankling hear but on the uther side of the mountain whair we went up it was ofell bad rodes. it snode a Sunday and Munday. the rest of the week we had good wether. we had a easy trip of it. we stopt every day for diner and all ways campt before nite. we got plenty of appels all the way. our march all the way from hear till we got back

[48] The editor did not locate Fleatown, but it is obviously near Crab Bottom which is in Highland County VA.

[49] Benjamin and Julia Bruce and family lived in Sand Hill District on a small farm. 1860 & 1870 Census.

was one hundred and ten miles. i dont feel enne tiarder that i did when i left. we seen no rebels. Averl had a fite at Rude Hill and i gess thay thout that thay wood come down by Monteray, then we wood drive them back but thay didant com that way so we didant see enne rebels in our hole trip. I seen Charley Bary and Will Dougherty to day. they are both well. Averls brigaid is hear. thay will leve in the morning.

i got a letter from Isaac yesterday. Thay was all well then. well it is gittin late and the mail will soon close and i will hafto stop. i hope these fue lins find you all well of your cold. thay leve me in good helth. giv mi love to all. no more but i remain your brother,

Joshua Winters.

Miss Anna M. Winters. Write soon. i wood rite more but it is late. Good by

DIARY. Mon Nov 15 1863. Clear. Averels begade left hear today. our wagon train was attacked today between hear and Berlington. Tues 17. clear today. i am on gard at the feed store in Petersburg. we got paid today. Wed 18. clear today. Thur 19. clear and nuthing goin on. Fri 20. pleasant day. nuthing strange. Sat 21. it has been a raining all day. i am on pickit on the Siniky rode today. Sun 22. clear today. Mon 23. pleasant day. Tues 24. pleasant day. Wed 25. pleasant day. i went five miles on the uther side of Moorefield with the train after hay. Thur 26. pleasant day. Fri. 27. pleasant day. Sat 28. i am on fitigue today. it raind. Sun 29. pleasant day. Mon 30. vary winday and cold. i am on pickit today. Tues Dec 1. vary winday today. Wed 2. i am on fatigue today. Thur 3. pleasant day. Fri 4. the sun is warm today.

[44] Petersburg Hardy Co West Va
December the 4th 1863

Dear Sister,

it is with plazer that i take mi pen in hand this beautiful day to answer your kind letter whitch i receved a fue days ago and to let you no that i am well and i hope if these fue lins reach you thay will find you all in good helth.

Well Anne, thair aint mutch news hear so i hardly no what to write about. i got a letter from Lonzo the uther day. thay was all well then Jake has a carbunkell on his rist. it was vary bad for to weeks but it is better now. this is a nice day. last week the wind blew so hard hear we was afraid it wood blow us away. i suppose the big meatin is still a goin on. i wood like to be at home now.

the news from the army for the last week or so is vary good. Grant has won a grate victory in Tennesee. Capterd five thousand prisners.[50] we expect to hear good news from the Army of the Potomac before long. Fredericksburg is now in our posesion. you wanted to no if the men of our regement that was taken at Moorefield had got back yet or not. thay ar not exchanged yet. we hurd from them the uther day. thair has been ten of them died since thay went to Richmond. Our prisners has a hard time of it thair now. it aint vary long now till thay commence to draft in West Va if thay dont volunteer. i dont cair how menne thay fetch. thair is sum gone home out of our regement to recrute but i dont think thay can fill our regement again. i wish thay cood. 9 munts will soon pass a way then marching and standing gard will be plaid out with me for awhile i think. we have nice warm qurters to stay in hear but it is a vary lonesom place. we ar tiard of it. Well i will bring mi letter to a close hopen you will write soon. Giv mi lov to all at home. No more at presant but still remain your brother.

Joshua Winters.

Miss Anna M. Winters

Write soon as you can. Good by

DIARY. Sat Dec 5 1863. plesant day i am on pickit gard to day on the New Crick rode. Sun 6. beautifill day. Mon 7. clear. Tues 8. clear. i have ben choppin wood to day. Wed 9. clear we started to Morefield after hay one oclock this morning, got back at 8 to night. Avrels begaid com to Petersburg to day. Thur 10. we left camp at 5 oclock this morning, waded the river, took the Frankling rode, marched 24 miles campt a littell after dark, stopt fur diner. all of Averls begaid is a long and the 14 Va, first Va. Fri 11. cool. on our march 5 oclock this morning stopt fur diner. we marched 20 mils, campt at dark, past through Frankling. all quiet to day, all tiard to night. Sat 12. it raind all day on our march 5 oclock this morning, campt thre in the eaving at Montaray. the rodes is vary muddy. it

[50] Probably Joshua had heard of the battle of Missionary Ridge on Nov 25.

raind all night.all vary wet. we com a 11 mils. Avrels begaid took the uther rode to day. Sun 13. clear to day started on our march this morning at a 11, our Co in the advance. drove the rebels out of Mac Doul[51] and campt thair. we com 10 mils. the pickits was fiard on. rained all night. Mon 14. sum rain to day. we laid all day at Mac Doul. the wind is vary high to night. we ar in 36 mils of Stanton. no word from Averl to day.

DIARY. Tue Dec 15 1863. clear to day we ar still at Macdoul. not mutch agoin on to day. later. the boys is all uneasey. we left 10 oclock to night. fell back 12 mils, campt 3 oclock at night. we waded runs crick we ar vary wet. Wed 16. we took up our line of march at sun up this morning for Crab Bottom, got thair and Campt at 1 oclock. i am on pickit at Crab Mils ford on our post. raind and sleted all night. cold. vary bad night. we com 10 mils to day. Thur 17. raind all day. i com of ov [off] gard vary wet. i have a bad cold. we ar in camp at Crab Bottom Mils. no word from Averl to day. Fri 18. winday and a snoing to day. we got ordors to march at 12 oclock. we got reddy and the order was counter manded. we hurd from Averl by the signal of to guns. it snode all night, cold. Sat 19. it is vary winday to day, snode all day. we ar still in camp at Crab Bottom. nothing strange to day. it was ofell cold all night. Sun 20. more plesant to day. the sun is a shining. sum snow to day. we got orders to be reddy to march 3 in the morning. Mon 21. we left Crab Bottom this morning at 4 oclock on the North Fork rode. we march 17 mils, campt. the rivers vary icey and bad. cold day. Tue 22. on our march this morning at 8 oclock, our regment in the rear. we marched 15 mils, no diner to day. vary bad rods. plesant day. Wed 23. on our march at 7 this morning. got to Petersburg at 3 in the eaving. all tiard. Thur 24. plesant day.

[45] To Joshua from Sister Anne

Sand Hill
December the 25, 1863

Dear Brother.

i drop Myself this Chrismas Morning to inform you that we are tolerable well hoping if these few lines reaches you may find you in

[51] McDowell, in now Highland County VA.

good health. Well Josse i recived your welcome letter and was glad to hear from you. Well there is not very much agoin at present but i think there will be plenty buissness this time next week. Well i was over at Aunt Pollys yesterdy. they are all well at presant. i haint got a letter from Lol since last week. He was well then. Well Josse i am goin to Wheeling next week if nothing happens maybe. Well i dont no what to rite about. We sent a boxe out to New Creek to the boys and when ever you come to Cumberlent, we will send somthing to you. Well Josse, Paps back is very bad and we have to help him. Tell Jake that Ally Baird[52] got his letter and was glad to hear from him. Well Josse I must bring my letter to a close by asking you to rite and to excuse me for not riting more. i will rite in a day or two again. we all send our love to you and hope you will get home soon.

from a dear Sister Anna Winters.

Sister Anna Winters

DIARY. Fri 25. plesant day. i have a vary bad cold. nothing goin on hear. Sat 26. Plesant day. Sun 27. sum rain to night.on duty to day unloden wagons. Mon 28. it raind to day. Tues 29. clear to day. Wed 30. i am on pickit to day on the North Fork rode. plesant day. Thur 31. we musterd for pay to day. it raind all day. all quiet and nuthing strange. lonesom place is this.

Memoranda.

We have not bin out of West Virginia this year.

We have bin under Kelley.

[Note in back of diary]

Brimfield, Peoria Co. Illinois[53]

---

[52] William C. and Margaret Baird lived near the Winters family. Mary Alice Baird was 12 or 13 in 1860. Census.

[53] Joshua's sister Lib and her husband, James Rogers, had moved there.

[In back of 1863 diary]:

List of Clothing

Jan 12- 2 shirts, 2 socks	$ 2.28
Jan 12- 2 pir drawers	1.00
Jan 22- 1 gum blankit	
Jan 19- trouses 1 socks	
May 17- 1 paged shoes	
Jume 1- one pair ov trousers	
July 26- one pair ov sode shues	1.05
Aug 14- one shirt 1 socks	1.78
Sept - pair trouser	3.55
sept 18- one blous not lind	2.40
Oct 26- 1 pair of socks	.32
Oct 26- 2 troues 2 socks	2.54
Nov 26- 1 woolin blanket	3.60
Nov 26- 1 pagued shoes	1.48
Nov 26- 2 shirts, knapsack	2.92
1 pair of trousers	3.55
	25.19
the amount of Clothing that i drew in 1863 is	$41.12

Price List of Clothen

Forge caps	.56
Covers	.18
Uniform coat privats	4.25
trouses	3.55
Flanel sack coat unlined	2.40
Lind	3.14
Flanel shirts	1.46
Drauers	.95
Stockings	.32
Bootes sewed	2.05
Pegged	1.48
Great Coats	9.58
Straps	.14
blankets woolen	3.60
painted	1.05
Ruber	2.85

[46] Petersburg West Va
December the 1th, 1864
[should be January 1, 1864]

Dear sister Allas,

it is with grate plazer that i take mi pen in hand to write you a fue lins but it wood give me more plazer to read a fue lins that you wood write to me. i am injoying good health at the presant and i hope these fue lins will find you all the same. well Alle this is new years and if i cood see you a runin around with your white hair a hanging about your shoulders i wood ask you for a new years gift. i caut a vary bad cold on our last raid but have got well of it now. if i was at home and thair was snow anuf we wood hitch up Juley and have a sleigh riden but maby you have a bo to take you a sleigh riden this eaving. if you have you must tell me of it. we can see snow in the mountains but thair is nun hear. i wrote Pap and Anne a letter a Chrismas. i suppose thay got it. tell me if thair is enne scool at Sand Hill this winter or not. i hope you have sinings a plenty to go to. i havant hurd from home for three weeks. i hope i will git a letter tonight. tell Easter that i will rite to hur soon. give mi love to all, Alle. i will close

from your brother Joshua Winters
To Alle E. Winters

do rite soon. the Wheeling battery will be hear to.

DIARY. 1864. Mr. Joshua Winters
Petersburg, Hardy County West Va
January the 1th 1864.

Steel not this book for fear of shame for in it is the owners name and on that day the Lord will say, whair is that book you took away.

Fri Jan 1, 1864. Petersburg, Hardy county West Va. it is vary winday and cold today. Sat 2. i am on pickit gard today on the North Fork rode.. it is vary winday and cold. Sun 3. the fort train was attacted and capterd at the jungtion 12 mils from hear.[1] Mon 4. it is snoing vary fast today. Tues 5. Clear and cold. i am on duty a cutten timber for the fort today. tonight at 7 oclock we got orders to pack up and be reddy to move at 2 in the morning. the order was countermanded. a grate deal of Commesarys stors are destroid. Wed 6. Clear today. the excitement is all over. Thur 7. cold today and a snoing tonight. Fri 8. i am on pickit gard on the Sinikey rode. vary cold today and tonight.

[47]

Petersburg West Va
January the 9th 1864

Dear sister,

it is with plazer that i seat miself this eaving to answer your letter. i wood of writtin sooner but the mail didant go from hear for a fue days so i thaut i wood write this eaving to let you no that i am well and i hope these fue lins will find you all in good helth. well i suppose you hurd of the wagon train a bein taken betwean hear and New Crick. thay got sum of the gards that was on the train but i gess thay onley got one or to of our regment. the rest got away. i gess thay was a lettel excited about the rail rode. thay thout the rebs was a goin to try it again. we was a lookin for them hear but thay didant trubel us. thay was betwean hear and New Crick. we coodant hear from New Crick a tall. we packed up and loud to leve hear the morning of the 6 at three in the morning. we had every thing reddy to burn when thair was a dispach cum to stay hear. we had destroid a good deal of grub before the order com. we thout we was a goin to git to leve hear but we was disapinted. i gess the rebs is all gone back and the scare is over. i hurd that the 15th was at Cumberland. i dont no how true it is. thair is rite smart of snow hear now. it has bin vary cold hear for the last week or so. i cant think of mutch to write. i have just written to Mary. i was on pickit last night and am to sleepy to write mutch today and i must git sum wood for tomorrow is Sunday. i was glad to hear you had sutch a good meetin at Sand Hill. well i beleve i will close mi short letter for this time. i will write soon a gain. giv mi love to all. no more from your brother,

Joshua Winters

---

[1] Long, 452. "Federal Calvary saw action in Hampshire and Hardy Counties, W. Va." on Jan 1.

Anna M. Winters. write soon. good by. you wanted to no how to drect the box if you send it. Mary will tell you the drections.

DIARY. Sat Jan 9, 1864. Winday and cold today. Sun 10. More plesant today. this eaving the wind raist and got colder. Mon 11. Clear. i am on gard on the Siniky rode today. Tues 12. this has bin a mild day. Wed 13. Plesant day. we got orders to knight if the long roll beat to fall in with our blankets on. Thur 14. Clear today. the snow is most all gon off. Fri 15. Plesant day. i am on gard at the fort. the rebs made thair apearnce in the gap. one reb killd. the 23 went out this eaving, got back this morning. the train com up today, larg gard with it.[2] Sat 16. plesant day. the train left for New Crick this morning. the 14 went with it as fur as Williamsport. Sun 17. Warm and plesant. Mon 18. Clouday. i am on fatigue today. Tues 19. our Co went on a scout through the gap today. the wind is vary heigh tonight. it blode severl houses down. Cold. Wed 20. plesant day. Thur 21. the wether is fair. Fri 22. warm today. i am on gard at head querters today. the wagon train com up today. Sat 23. beautifill day.

[48] [From Anna to Joshua] Sand Hill

Marshall Co. West Va.

January 24, 1864

Dear brother,

it is with pleasur that i take up my pen to inform you that we are all in good health and do hope you are the same. Well, Lol got home last night. he is well and looks hearty. Well you might be sure that there aint much new to rite or i wood not rite on so small a piece of paper. there was a sining at Sand Hill meeting house a Saturday night but i was not there. there was preaching there on Thursday and i went and i thought i wood not go a Saturday night. we had a dreadful deep snow last week but it is about all gone now. Well i got a letter from Lib and Jim yesterday Evening. they are well and have moved to themselves. Well there is a sining at Alexandrie

[2] Long, 455, "Fighting was confined to a skirmish near Petersburg, W. Va." Jan 15.

Campell[3] this week but i dont think i will trouble myself a goin. i dont ceare about going such place myself. Well we wood of sent your box a good wheil ago but the water was up bad. we could not get to town in the wagon. we will send it next week if nothing happenes. excuse this short letter and i will rite more next time. answer soon. From your sister

Anna M. Winters

to Joshua Winters. rite as soon as you can and tell us all the news.

DIARY. Sun Jan 24. Clear and winday. Mon 25. Warm wether for the time of year. i am on fatigue today in the fort. Tues 26. it is vary winday today. Wed 27. Calm to day. Thurs 28. Clear and warm. our regment left Camp this morning with 4 day ratiuns on the New Crick rode. we got to the junction, 12 mils, eat our diner, then orderd back. got in to camp at dark. Fri 29. vary warm. i am on pickit. the 29 left this morning to go to the Morefield junction to blockkade the rode over the mountain and to stay thair till the train past up and down. Sat 30. Cloudy and driseln rain to day. the train was taken today betwean Petersburg and Berlington.[4] Sun 31. drizling rain. we avacuated Petersburg this morning at one oclock. on the rode through Shels Gap, struck the northwestern rode at Greanland Gap. our regment got thair at 9 oclock, wated thair till the rest got up. left thair at 3, went 4 mils and campt at dark. bad rodes, dark nights.

Monday Feb 1, 1864. on our march at one this morning. stopt at day lite for breckfist. got in to mils of New Crick at diner time then went on the hill above New Crick and campt. i am on pickit tonight, the rode vary mudy. we com 42 mils yesterday and today. the rebs folard us up. Tues 2. laid on the hill all day. trups passin west on the rail rode. we left New Crick at dark, got to Berlington at day light. most all of the regment a stragglin. vary dark. i stopt in a town house. grate exitement at New Crick. we packed our

---

[3] Alexander H. and Mary A. Campbell and a large family lived in the area near the Winters families. 1860 Census.

[4] Long, 458,459: "Cavalry skirmished at Medley, W. Va." on Jan 29. On Jan 30, "Action included skirmishing ... at Medly, W. Va." Medley is a village just east of Greenland Gap, north of Petersburg.

knapsacks. Wed 3. nice day. we campt on the hill above Burlington rode. thair all night. three regments of our begaid moved towards Morefield and to regments of Avarls begaid, the 4 Va, and to peces of artilery com up tonight. Thurs 4. nice day but raind sum tonight. all quiet hear. Fri 5. Clear today. all the trups com back from Morefield to Berlington and campt for the night. thay was in sight of the rebel train. it raind tonight. Sat 6. on our march earley this morning for New Crick, got within 2 mils of New Crick and campt at 1 oclock. the 14 Va staid at Berlington. the rods vary muddy. Sun 7. vary winday today. i washed mi clothes. Muligan reveued the 139 Pennsylvania. Mon 8. Clear and vary winday today. we drove wedge tents today. Tues 9. Clear but still winday. Wed 10. Clear. we got paid today for to munts.

[49]

New Crick West Va
February the 10th 1864

Dear Sister,

it is with plazer that i seat mi self this eaving to let you no that i am well and i hope that these fue lins will find you all injoying good helth. well Anne your letter com to hand at last and Nancy's today. Thay was a good while on the rode. it went to Martainsburg then com back hear. well the raid is over and we ar in camp a gain at New Crick. we got a way safe from Petersburg and i am glad of it for i was tiard of that place. thay had us pretty well pennd up but old Josse slipt out. we had a vary hard march till we got hear. then we went out to Burlington. the rodes was vary muddy and we had to pack our knapsacks. it went hard on us for we wasant use to it but we was so glad to git a way from Petersburg we didant mindit. i hope we will stay hear till spring. thair is a good menne of our regement a reinlisting now. thair is sumthing like 200 reinlisted. it is pretty wether hear now onley it is winday. we got paid to day for to munts.

well i hurd that Mother was sick. i want you to write as soon as you can and tell me how she is gittin. i was glad to hear of Lonzo a gittin home. well Anne i believe i have written all the news that i can think of. tell Nancy that i will answer hur letter soon. mi love to you all. i hope this letter will find you all in as good a helth as it leves me. i will close for the presant. from your brother

Joshua Winters

rite soon. Good by　　to Miss Anne M. Winters

DIARY. Thurs Feb 11, 1864. plesant day. i was out in the country to day. Fri 12. plesant day. Sat 13. plesant day. i am on duty today. Sun 14. clear. Tues 16. clear and winday. ofell cold. Wed 17. clear and winday, ofell cold. Fri 19. we left camp this eaving and went to the woods, staid all night.

[50] [From Anna M. Winters to Joshua]

Sand Hill Marshall Co. West Va
[about 20] February [1864]

Dear brother,

it is with pleasure that i take up my pen this morning to let you no that we are in good Health and hope that these few lines may find you well. we received your letter this week and was glad to hear from you and that you had got off safe. there is great talk of the war being over since the last raid. it was in the papers that your regiment had give them a fight. Well, Josse, Lol got home ten Dayes and then when he went to Wheeling to start the cars was not running and he came and started another day and went back again and we did not hear what time he got started. we have got no letter from him since he left but i think i will get one this evening. Well Josse, i rote a letter to you and sent it will be two weeks against Tuesday next but i suppose it did not go. Pap was going to Fulton this morning and if he would of told me last night i could of rote your letter in some decency. i did not no it till this morning or i would of rote more. But these few lines will let you no that we have not forgot you yet. Well, we got your bootes half solled and took them to Wheeling but i dont no wether she has sent them yet or not. we could of sent you a boxe but they said the first virginia was coming to Wheeling.

i must bring these few lines to a close by asking you to rite. Mother and Pap and the rest send their love to you.

No more at this time from your Sister,

Annie Winters

To Brother Joshua Winters
Please to rite soon

DIARY. Fri Feb 20, 1864. we left New Crick at 6 this eaving on the cars for Wheeling. thair was 100 rouns of artillry fiard when we left. Sun 21. we arived in Wheeling 2 oclock this eaving, eat our diner at the depo, then marched in to the [ethemen]. our regment was dismisst for the night. Mon 22. We met at one this eaving and praided the streets of Wheeling at 5. we marched to the Washington Hall[5], got our supper, thair was spekin. Tues 23. i went out home today, stopt at Coffee Town for a sining, got home at 11 at night. Wed 24. out on Sand Hill today. Plesant day. Thurs 25. went to Wheeling today, had a good time. plesant day. Fri 26. com home today out on the cars. plesant day. Sat 27. rode down on Sand Hill today. clear day. Sun 28. raind today. i was riden around today. Mon 29. i went to Wheeling today. we musterd for pay. liveley time thair.

Tues March 1, 1864. snoing today. i rode out and staid all night. Wed 2. Clear. i was at a party tonight at Dans.[6] Thurs 3. Clear today. halld sum straw today. the snow is a goin of vary fast. Fri 4. Clear and winday. i was a choppin sum today. Sat 5. raining today. i was out a ridin today. Sun 6. Clear today. i was at church at Sand Hill today. Mon 7. Clear. i was at the shop today. Tues 8. plesant day. i was at Unkell Alberts[7] today. Wed 9. plesant day. i halled stone in the forenoon today and rode out this eaving, away to night. Thurs 10. raind all day. Fri 11. raind today. i was at a sining tonight at Adsonn.[8] Sat 12. Clear. i was out a ridin today. Joseh Blake[9] was hear last night. Sun 13. it raind all day hard. . Mon 14. damp. i went to Wheeling today, at a speeking tonight at Washington Hall. it snode today. Tues 15. i com home today. the rods is vary muddy. went to the sining at Coffee Town. Sun 20. i was at Haneytown[10] to preachin today, vary cold. Mon 21. i was at a partey tonight. plesant day. Tues 22. winday today. i was at a oster supper tonight at Coffee Town. Thurs 24.i was at a sining on Sand Hill tonight. Sun 27. i was at church at Sand Hill today. Mon 28. i com in to Wheeling

---

[5] Washington Hall, built in 1852, was an important center in Wheeling and was the state capitol of West Virginia when it burned in 1875. McConnell, 40-44.

[6] Probably his first cousin, Daniel Winters, (wife Mary Jane Rodgers) who lived in the area.

[7] Albert Davis, brother of Joshua's mother, who lived with his wife, Mary (Rodefer) Davis, on Big Wheeling Creek, Sand Hill District. The editor is their descendant.

[8] Unknown.

[9] If this was Joshua Blake, Joshua's future father-in-law, it is reasonable that he should visit. One wonders why he mispelled "Joshua" though, his own name. There were Joseph Blakes but it was more likely to be Joshua, who lived a few miles away and was a friend and relative of Joshua's father.

[10] Haneytown, mentioned frequently, is now known as Dallas and was the nearest "town".

today. Tues 29. went in a hack[11] to Trydelphia today. a few of us had a good time. raind all day. Wed 30. i went home today and back this eaving. it raind vary hard all day. had a good time. Thurs 31. we was reddy to leve today then put it of.

Fri April 1 1864. we left Wheeling this eaving at 3 oclock in the cars. had a vary tiresom ride of it. raind all day. Sat 2. we arived at Webster this morning at 9 oclock, all tiard. we campt in a mill. it raind all day. Sun 3. Cloudy today. the 14 Va and the Wheeling battery arived hear this morning and stoard all our bagage today. i have bin walking up and down the rail rode. vary lonesom today.

[51] Webster. West Va.
Aprile the 3th 1864

Dear Sister,

it is with plazer that i seat mi self this morning to let you no that i am well and i hope that these fue lins will find you all injoying the same blessing. well we left Wheeling a Friday eaving and we got hear a Satterday morning at 9 oclock. thair was but one car for a Co. and thair was no seats in them. we was vary mutch crowded. we had no rume to sleep. it was the tiresomest ride that we ever had. we are now campt at Webster on the North Western railrode. our regement is in a mill. our Co. is in the 4th story of the mill.

we never was in this part of the cuntry before and i tell you it is not a pretty place. the 14th Va infantry arrived hear this morning and the Wheeling battery, thay say the 12, is a cumin. i gess we will be formed in a bregade hear and Curnel Thoburn[12] will be our bregade Commander. the boys all thinks that we will go to Bevely. that is 42 miles from hear. it is not surtin whether we will go thair or not. i hope the mud will dry up first. it has bin araining for to days hear, vary muddy. this day is clouday. me and to more is out on the side of a hill writing by a fire. well me and Will got back to Wheeling safe the day we was out home but we was vary mudday. i wood of went home and staid a while longer but i thout i had

[11] Probably a hired, horse-drawn buggy or wagon.

[12] Colonel Joseph Thoburn originally commanded the first West Virginia Regiment. He led the second brigade in Sullivan's Division in the Valley Campaign in 1864 and was killed at Cedar Creek in October. Strother, 244. Joshua apparently respected him highly.

better com with the regement sins i havant long to stay. Jake is not hear yet. thair was a good menny boys left back. everything goes like it ust to. it will be hard on us for a fue days i recon. i want you to write soon and tell me all the news and if enne boddy has said enne thing a bout me sins i left let me no it. well i believe i will close for this time. you will hear from me soon again. giv mi love to all from your brother

Joshua Winters

Anna M. Winters. Good by. write soon. this will leve hear on the 4 of Aprile. let me no all that is a goin on.

DIARY. Sun Apr 3, 1864. Cloudy to day the 14 Va. and the Wheeling battery arived hear this morning we stoard all our bagage today. i have bin walking up and down the rail rode vary lonesom today. Mon 4. it raind all day the 15 Va. arived hear this morning. it is vary muddy hear. Our Co. was detaild for duty this eaving. Tue 5. clear and plesant. to regments of Pennsylvania reservs arived hear today. Co C of the 1th got hear this eaving. Wed 6. clear today. trups still a cumin in. Thur 7. this has bin a warm day. Fri 8. plesant day. no news today. we had regmental inspection and dres praid today. Sat 9. it raind studdy all day and night. nuthing strange today. Sun 10. this has bin a beauti full day till eaving then it raind. Mon 11. sum rain today. i moved out of the mill on the side of a hill today. thair was a regment of cavery past hear on the cars to day.

[52] To Miss Eliza A. Winters[13]

Webster, West Va.
Aprile the 12th 1864

Dear Sister,

it is with plazer that i seat mi self to pen you a fue lins to let you no that i am well and i hope that these fue lins will find you a settin in the rocking chair with clean hans and face drest up a readin sum pretty story like a lady. i hope your hans wont be soild by washing the dishes.

well Alle, the last day that i was at home i thout i wood of been

[13] Eliza Alice, called Alice, Joshua's youngest sister, was fourteen at this time.

back again. we got in Wheeling a bout dark. i think thair was sum mud on us when we got in. we made the honeys travell in a hurry. it aint long till i will bee back and mabey the war will be over a gainst that time.

i havant bin on dutty since we com out thair so no pickit to do hear. well Alle, as news is scarce i will haft to close by asking you to write soon. you must be a good girl and do whatever Mother tells you and i will by you a nice presant when i come home. so no more at presant but still remain your brother

Joshua Winters

to Miss Alle E. Winters. write soon. good by.
direct to Webster W Va

DIARY. Tue Apr 12, 1864. it has raind most all day. the 12 Va. com back from Beverly today. Wed 13. it raind today, got sum colder this eaving. Thur 14. Clear today and sum colder. thair was sum trups past hear today goin toards Clarksburg. Fri 15. it driseld rain this eaving. we had begaid inspection today. Sat 16. it is damp this morning an snode vary fast this eaving. thair was sum of the first Va Cavery past hear today. Sun 17. it spit snow and sprinkeld rain today. we had dres praid this eaving. Mon 18. this is a plesant day. we moved our camp in a vary pretty place. i am on gard tonight at head qurters. Tue 19. plesant day. thair was battaling drill and dress praid today. it is rite cold tonight. Wed 20. nice day. got marching orders this eaving. broke up camp at 8 tonight, went over to Grafton, rode thair till 12 then returned to camp, put up our tents again. i wrote home tonight. dres praid this eaving. Thur 21. plesant day. we got on the cars at Grafton at 12 oclock today for Martainsburg. the cars was crouded. we put in a vary unplesant night. Fri 22. we arived at Martinsburg at three oclock this eaving. Camp in a nice place one mile from the town. Sat 23. it has bin vary warm today. i washed mi cloes. i was over in Martainsburg today. Sun 24. Clear today. we had Co drill this fournoon and battaling drill this eaving. thair was a regement and a battery left hear today on a 4 day scout up the valley. Tues 26. Clear today. we had regemental inspection and Co drill and dress praid today. Wed 27. it is winday and cold today. thair was Co drill in the fournoon. thair was generl revew this eaving of all the trups that is hear. Mager Generl Seagul[14] and Mager Generl Stalk[15] reveud us. the 6 Va Cavery left hear this eaving on the cars west. Thur 28. this has bin a plesant day. thair was Co drill and battaling drill today. thair was sum trups com hear today. we got orders to march in the morning. Fri 29. vary warm. all the trups at Martainsburg started up the valley this morning under the command of Seagul, Stalk, Cuverling.[16] marched slo. campt 4 in the eaving at Bunker HIll. packed 5 days grub in our knapsacks. Sat 30. we mustered for pay earley this morning. it raind all eaving. thair was sum trups com up today. we laid at Bunker HIll all day. we had inspection of knapsacks today.

[53] Bunker Hill Virginia
April the 30the 1864

Dear sister,

it is with plazer that i take mi pen in hand this eaving to let you no that i am well at preseant and i hope that these fue lins will find you all injoying good helth. i receved your letter this morning and was glad to hear from you both. we left Martainsburg yesterday morning, up the valley. we packed our knapsacks for five days, grub on our backs. it was vary warm but we marched slow. we com 10 mils, campt 4 in the eaving. we ar now in 12 mils of Winchester. i beleve thair is about ten thousand hear all together. thair is more a cumin. Generl Seagel is along and Generl Suveland, and i forget the uther Generls name that has the Cavery. We ar in Thoburns begaid. perhaps we will lay hear for a fue days. perhaps we will move on when the rest of the force gets up hear. we may have a fite in this valley. it is hard to tell but i think not for a week or so. thirty days will make a big change in this war i think. i suppose the Potomac Armey is a moveing or els we woodant advance up this valley. well it is a raining vary hard and studdy this eaving. i am glad we aint a marchin today. when you write again tell me whair the 15 was when

---

[14] Major General Franz Sigel, a German immigrant. He assumed command of the Federal Department of West Virginia from Brig. General Benjamin F. Kelley on March 10. Long, 473.

[15] Major General Julius Stahel was a favorite of Sigel. Strother, 217.

[16] Jeremiah C. Sullivan served under Shields in the Valley of Virginia in 1862, and returned to Virginia to lead the First Infantry Brigade under Sigel and Hunter. Strother, 208. Joshua eventually improved in spelling his name.

you hurd from them. i havant hurd whair thay ar for to weeks. i seen Jim Marsh. he is hear. he looks about like he ust to. i was glad to hear that Pap had got through plowing for i was afraid it wood make his leg wors. well i beleve i will close for this time by askin you to write as soon as you can. this is a answer to your letter and Easters both, from

Your Brother Joshua Winters

Anna M. Winters, Easter R. Winters. Giv mi love to Pap, Mother, Alle and both of you.

---------- ---------- ---------- ------------

well Easter, when was Bille up? Anna when did you hear from John? Alle, how is Jimmie?[17] i wood like to hear from Lizabeth.[18] i hope she is better. well it still rains. Jake is well. i will write soon again and you all do the same. so good bye for the presant time. this will leve hear the 1st day if May

----

Ego Amo Too Ego Amo Too

----

i want to no if you no the meaning of this word.

i want to no if you no the meaning of this word

[A loose piece of paper stuck in the pages of the diary says, in Joshua's handwriting]:

Ego Amo Too

I Love you

----

i receved six dolars from home in 1864

[17] William Dague, who eventually married Easter, and James Dague who eventually married Alle. John is unknown unless it is John Cruson. Anna did not marry.

[18] James Rogers was discharged for disability in April 1863 and the family moved to Peoria County IL. Elizabeth had just given birth to her second son at this time but apparently they didn't discuss such delicate matters.

DIARY. Sun May 1 1864. we left Bunker Hill 10 this morning, our regement in the rear. Past through Winchester to mile then campt. marched 14 mils. nice day. Co. F, Co. K, Co. G campt with the train for gards one mile from the regment. stopt for diner today. Mon 2. we had batalling drill this fournoon. this eaving playing fite. it raind this eaving. Generl Seagell drilld the begaid. Tues May 3. Clear today. we moved to our regment today. we had battalling drill and dress praid this eaving. we sent our knapsacks back to Martainsburg tonight. Wed 4. plesant day. we had Co drill, battaling drill, dress praid today. Our Cavery capterd 25 rebs at Strawsburg today. i am on gard tonight. Thur 5. i was on gard all day. thair was drill today. a warm day.

[54]

Camp First West Va Infantry
Near Winchester Va
May the 5th 1864

Dear Sister,

it is with plazer that i take mi pen in hand this warm eaving for the purpis of answering your kind letter whitch i received five minits ago and was glad to hear that you was all well and that Lib is better and i hope if these fue lins reach you thay will find you all as thay leve me, that is in good helth. Well Anne we arived hear the first day of this month. we ar campt one mile on the uther side of town on the second battell ground 2 miles from the first one. it is a vary pretty place to drill whitch thay keep us at 4 or 5 hours every day. i do hate to drill these hot days.

our Cavary had a littel fuss yesterday up the valley. thay caut 26 rebs. thay got a fue wagons from us the uther day betwean hear and Martainsburg. thay say thay dashed in to Martainsburg last night and captered sum of our min.[19] i dont no whether it is so or not. it is nuthing but Cavary and thay cant hurt us mutch. we have a good menne Cavary hear and thay will fetch them at sum of thair dashes. we have a pretty large force hear. it is hard to tell what day we will move. it is one mile to the army of the Potomac. if the rebs get whipt we will go on and if not we will fall back. every thing looks natcherl hear. as we past through Winchester a Sunday eaving thair

[19] Long, op. cit., does not mention these events. The Battle of the Wilderness is getting underway.

was one house waved thair hanker chief. it is vary warm in day light but cold at nights. we have sent our knapsacks and all our baggage back but our blankets. Jake Sols went to the hospittell a Tuesday. he has the feaver. Charley and Harson Blake[20] told me that Will went to the hospittell at Frederick Citty with the small pox or the chicken pox, thay didn't no whitch. Charley said he had a furlow to go to Philidelphia but i dont no what he went fur. i got a letter from you and Easter and i answered it at Bunker Hill. when you write tell me if you got it. the boys aint wrote to me since i saw them at Webster. i hope you girls will fill your offices well. i will close for the presant. mi love to you all. i hope to hear from you as soon as possibel. no more at presant

Joshua Winters

to Sister Anna M. Winters. Good by.

DIARY. Fri May 6. vary hot today. we had scrumish drill today and begaid drill this eaving. Seagell and Suterland both was presant. Sat 7. warm today. we had scurmish drill in the morning. thay giv us this eaving for to wash. thair was dress praid this eaving. Sun 8. plesant day. thair was Co inspection and dress praid today. i am not vary well this eaving. Mon 9. vary warm today. Seagels divishion took up thair line of march this morning from Winchester at 7 oclock. up the valley. went 15 mils, campt at Cedar Crick 4 in the eaving. past through Curnstown, Newtown, Midelltown. all vary tiard. Thur 10. warm today. we had batalling drill this eaving. it commenced to rain at dark. We laid hear all day till the bridg was bilt over Cedar Crick. Wed 11. Clouday and sum rain. we ar on our march this morning at 6, past through Strawsburg, campt near Woodstock. we marched 14 mils today. our Co. and Co. K went on pickit. we was alarmed five times tonight. raind all night. marched past camp 3 in eaving. Thur 12. it raind most all day and night. we are still on gard. i com off today. thair was no alarm tonight on our post. Fri 13. we was releved of our gard this morning. our begaid went on a scout today on difernt rodes. our regement went 5 mils to the right of Wood-

---

[20] Robert Harrison Blake, born in 1839, son of Robert and Nancy (Campbell) Blake, was called Harrison. He was related to Joshua's future wife. The others are probably Charles Berry and William Daugherty.

stock. got back about 6 this eaving. it raind all day and night. Sat 14. we left Woodstock this morning at 11 oclock. three regements of infantry, sum cavery, met the rebs at Mount Jackson, drove them to New Market, shelld them thair. thay advanced on us at dark. the infantry drove them back. all vary tiard. it raind all day and night.

Sun 15. it still rains hard. the cananading commenced earley this morning. the rest of our force com up this morning. infantry got ingaged about the midil of the day. thay drove us hard to Rudes Hill, stopt thair. we crost the bridg then burnt it, then marched on back, our regement in the rear. got to Edenburg at daylight, burnt the bridg, then our regement took the advance. got to Cedar Crick at dark and campt. all giv out.[21] Mon 16. i am on gard tonight. the distance from New Market to Cedar Crick is ___. Tues 17. clear today. we moved acrost Cedar Crick and campt. all vary tiard today. i com off of gard this eaving. the wounded was sent back to Martainsburg today. Wed 18. it raind today. the 12 Va and the 34 Md went out to Fishers Hill today on pickit duty.

[55] Camp near Strawsburg at Cedar Crick
Dear Sister, May the 18th 1864

it is with plazer that i seat mi self this morning to let you no that i am well at presant and i hope these fue lins will find you all well. i wood of writtin sooner but the mail woodant go. we had a vary hard fite a Sunday the 15th and we fell back hear about 20 mils. we had a hard march or to since i wrote last. well i wont tell you enne thing about the fite[22] for it is hard to tell whether this letter will go or not. I havant hurd from Sols[23] since he went to the hospittell nor i havant hurd from the 15 Va since you rote last. well it is no use to write mutch for mabe it will never reach you and this will let you no that i got through safe and am well so i will close for this time. Write soon and drect to Martainsburg

mi love to you all. good by. From Joshua Winters

i will write as soon as i can again

---

[21] Long, 501-502: May 14, skirmish at Rude's Hill. May 15, Battle of New Market.

[22] Sigel's Federal Troops suffered a sharp defeat at New Market and retreated to Strasburg. The Federals suffered 831 total casualities, the Confederates 577, dead, missing and wounded. Long, May 15, 502.

[23] Jacob Soles.

DIARY. Thur May 19. Clear today. we had regemental inspection. Fri 20. Clear and warm. thair was sum reinforcements to com up today. the right wing of our regement was working on brestworks this eaving. Sat 21. Clear today. we had Co. drill this morning and this eaving. Sun 22. Clear and plesant. we had Co. inspection today. Generl Hunter[24] took command of this department today. Mon 23. Clear today. we had regemental inspection this morning. this eaving we moved camp about one mile and drawd 10 days rations for a march. Tues 24. it is vary warm. i went as a gard with a wagon out to the pickits with aminition, 6 mils. we drew 100 rounds of cattridgers today. our knap sacks got hear today. it lighting and thundard and raind this eaving. Wed 25. warm today. thair was a thunder storm this eaving. we turned our Co.s 100 rouns of the cattridgers over today. Thur 26. warm and sultry today. the Armey of the Shenadoor started on the march this morning, went 15 mils, campt at Woodstock. packed our knapsacks. it rained this eaving. Fri 27. Clear today. we fell in line this morning at daylight, stood 15 minits. nuthing strange a goin on. Sat 28. warm today. we had Co. drill this morning. thair was sum trups arived hear this eaving. our min is a foragin for every thing to eat. Sun 29. plesant day. we left Woodstock this morning at 5. marched slo to Rude hill, a distance of 15 mils. campt 4 in the eaving. our cavery drove the rebs out of Newtown.[25] Mon 30. plesant day. nuthing strange today. our Co. went on pickit today. we hurd that som of our trains was capterd at Newtown. Tues 31. plesant day. we ar on pickit 2 mils from camp. we have nuthing to eat today. we was releved at dark this eaving.

Wed June 1 1864. vary warm today. we had Co. drill. we got marchin orders this eaving. Thur 2. raind today. we left New Market at 5 and campt at 4 in the eaving at Harrisnburg. the rebs shot 6 times at our min. we hear artillary. we marched 20 mils, all tiard and hungary. we captered som rebs hear. Fri 3. Clear today. we laid at Harisinburg all day. no news today. Sat 4. vary warm. we left Harisinburg this morning on the rode to Port Republic. got thair at

---

[24] Major General David Hunter took over the command from Sigel in the Department of West Virginia on May 21, after Sigel's failure in recent action. Long, 506.

[25] Long, 510; May 29, there were skirmishes at Newtown, Va.

dark, campt. our regement in the rear. nuthing to eat.[26]

[There are no more diary entries during June or until the last day of July. Joshua was wounded in the right hand, probably on June 5.[27] From his next letter we see that he walked, with his wounded hand, from Staunton VA to near Grafton WV before he was transported by train the remaining distance to the Parkersburg General Hospital.

Muster records show Joshua absent during June, July and August, with the notation "In hospital wounded". The 1890 Federal Special Schedule for Surviving Soldiers... indicates Joshua had a "gunshot wound to hand".

Joshua's granddaughter, Mary Winters, remembers her grandmother speaking of the injury. She believes it was an accident occurring while Joshua was "biting a bullet" that exploded in his hand, and was not the result of enemy fire. She said that the injury to his little finger was evident all his life. Joshua explained the wound in his following letter as being caused by a ball passing through his hand near the base of his thumb and then through his little finger, without breaking any bones.][28]

---

[26] Long, 515, Saturday June 4; "As Hunter's Federals advanced in the Shenandoah there was fighting at Port Republic and Harrisonburg, Va."

[27] Long, 516, June 5, Sunday, 1864:

"Confederates under W.E. 'Grumble' Jones moved to stop Hunters's destructive raid in the Shenandoah. With about 5600 men in all, Jones met Hunter's main force of around 8500 at Piedmont, about seven miles southwest of Port Republic. Charges and countercharges lasted until mid-afternoon, when Federal Infantry and Cavalry routed the southern troops. Jones was killed in the engagement. Hunter moved on into Staunton to continue his raids.... Federals lost around 780 men and the Confederates about 1600, of which around 1000 were captured." June 6, Monday.... "Federal troops under Hunter occupied Staunton, an important operational center in the Shenandoah."

Strother, 242-246, gives a detailed account of the activities on June 5. Gen. Stahel was wounded in the arm by a piece of shell. Rebel Gen. Jones was killed. The success of this engagement "had wiped out the disgrace of New Market" in the eyes of the celebrating troops. "Sullivan had three horses shot under him and won laurels for gallantry today."

[28] D. Stephen Haynes of Fairmont WV who has expertise in the field of Civil War weaponry, has explained how this accident probably happened. "Soldiers who used the muzzleloader as a weapon generally used pre-formed cartridges to facilitate the rapid firing of the weapon. These cartridges were constructed by rolling paper around

[56] Parkersburg, West Va
June the 24th 1864

Dear Sister,

it is with plazer that i take my pen in hand this morning to let you no that i am well at presant and i hope that these fue lins will find you all the same. Well Anne i received your letter of the 27th of May at Stanton. i outt to of answered it sooner. we got hear last Sunday.[29] we walked from Stanton to Webster. it was 150 miles. i like this place vary well. we ar gittin along vary well. well the ward that i stay in is all Virginians. thair is to out of mi Co. hear so i dont git lonesom. we can go to town every day if we want to. mi hand is a gittin well vary fast. it dont pane me enne now. it is mi rite hand. i am a writin with it and i dont recon you can read it. thair was no bones hurt. the ball went in the fleche part of mi thum betwean mi rist and the first joint, com out near the hart of mi hand, went through the fleche part of mi littel finger betwean the first and second joint. i am vary glad that i got off so safe. we have all sent in for a furlow but it may be a munth before we get them. i seen Isaac and Lonzo at Stanton. thay was both well and all the rest of the Sand Hill boys. well i will get clear of sum of the hard marches this summer and can lay in the shade hear and think about them a marchin.

write soon and tell me all the news and what is a goin on the 4th of July. you will haft to scuse this bad writin. i think i can do better the next time. i will close for the presant. write soon. direct your letter to Parkersburg U G hospittell. Joshua Winters

to his Sister Anne M. Winters mi love to you all. good by.

---

a wooden pin to form a tube. One end was closed by twisting the paper and then a measured amount of powder was poured into the tube. A lead shot was then placed on top of the powder and the tube was closed by twisting the other end. In loading the muzzleloader, the soldier would obtain a cartridge from his cartridge case and bite off the twisted end of the tube nearest the powder. He would then pour the powder down the barrel followed by the ball and a wad of paper. On occasion, soldiers would reload so rapidly that the hot embers remaining in the barrel from the previous shot would be fanned by the draft created by the powder falling down the barrel, and would ignite the fresh powder prematurely. Since the ball and wadding would still be in position over the muzzle of the rifle, the ball would be fired out of the hand, sometimes with dire consequences."

[29] "Last Sunday" would have been June 19. Joshua required just two weeks to walk the 150 miles from Staunton to Webster, and be transported to Parkersburg by rail.

[57] Parkersburg, West Va
July the 6th 1864

Dear Sister,

it is with pleasure that i take mi pen in hand to let you no that i am well at presant and i hope these fue lins will find you all well. Well Anna, i receved your letter that you sent hear to me and i was glad to hear from you all. i wood of answered it sooner but i had just put one in the office for you the day before i got yours, then i thout i woodant write for a day or to. Well, the first Va com up the river last night. thay took the cars this morning and went on toards Martainsburg. i didant get to see Jake. he will be hear today. i gess he is with the train. i was luckey a gittin away from them when i did for thay had a hard time. thay ar all most run down and starved. thay hadant mutch to eat. the 15th is at Charleston [W. Va.]. perhaps thay will be a past hear in a day or so. Well the 4th is a past. when you write tell me what was goin on at Sand Hill. Well, mi hand is still a gittin better but i cant write vary well with it yet. it will be all right again in a fue days. well it is prutty near diner time and i musant miss that, you no, so i will close for this time. i will write soon again.

Joshua Winters

to sister Anna M. Winters
mi love to you all. good by write soon

[58] Parkersburg, West Va
July the 17th 1864

dear sister,

it is with plazer that i take mi pen in hand this saboth morning to write you a fue lins to let you no that i am well at presant and i hope these fue lines will find you all the same. Well Anna, i receved your letter yesterday and i was glad to hear from you and to hear that you was all well. i am still a bummin at the hospittal. mi hand is well. i think i will go to the regement this week. well if i had a node that thair was enne thing a goin on at Sand Hill the 4th i wood of been home if i had to run off. well, i cant think of enne thing to write about. i will write as soon as i get to the regement. Isaac will write a fue lins. mi pen is bad. i will close. Drect to Martainsburg

Joshua Winters

to Anne M. Winters

[On the same letter, from Joshua's brother, Isaac.][30]

Parkersburg West Va.
July the 17the 1864

Dear Sister,

it is with pleasuer that i take my pen in hand to let you no that i am in good health at present and i hope that these few lines may find you all in good health. When i come here i was rite sick but i have got well again. My back is vary weake yet but it will be all rite in 2 or 3 days. well, i cant think of enything to rite. i rote Mother on Friday. Good by rite soon.

I.D. Winters

to Anney M. Winters

DIARY. Sunday July 31 1864. warm today. Harvey[31] and West and miself crost the Ohio in a skift and staid all day.

[59] to Alis E. Winters

Parkersburg, West Va.
August the 3th 1864

Dear Sister,

it is with plazer that i seat mi self this eaving to write you a fue lines to let you no that i am well and i hope that these fue lins will find you all in good helth. Isaac and Harvey is hear yet. thay ar both well but we cant git away. i tried to git away last week but i coodant. then i tried this week again but thay wont let us go for ten days. i have not hurd from them since thay had the fite, nor i havant hurd from Alonzo yet. i wood like to hear from him. the last letter that i received from home was dated 12 of July. it rained vary hard hear all day yesterday. well thair is nuthing to write about hear so this will

---

[30] Isaac D. Winters, Sgt. and later Second Lieutenant, belonged to Co. I, 15th Regiment, W. Va. Volunteers. His official Muster Roll shows that he was "absent sick" in July-August. He was admitted to the Parkersburg General Hospital on July 9, returned to his unit on Sept 7. He was therefore able to spend some time with his brother.

[31] (William) Harvey Winters, cousin of Joshua, was mustered into Company I of the Fifteenth Regiment, Company I, at the same time as Joshua's brothers. He served his entire tour of duty. Apparently he was wounded or ill since he was in the hospital with his cousins. We do not know who West was. Harvey had a brother, John Wesley Winters, who could have been visiting.

let you no that we ar all well, so i will close hopin to hear from you all soon. from your brother,

Joshua Winters

Miss Alis E. Winters

mi love to you all. it aint long till i will bee home to stay.

[60] Parkersburg West Va.
August the 5th 1864

Dear Sister,

it is with plazer that i write these fue lins to you to let you no that i am well and i hope these fue lins will find you all injoying good helth. well i receved your letter dated the 30th of July and i was glad to hear from you. i am a gittin vary tiard of this place but thay wont let no one go to the regement now. i havant hurd from Alonzo yet. the war noos has bin good for a fue days. Isaac is well. i will close. this is from your brother

Joshua Winters

to Anne M. Winters mi love to you all
good by write soon

DIARY. Sat Aug 6. all the malitia was calld out today. Sun 7. the malitia went in camp today one mile from Parkersburgh. Wed 10. Left the hospittal at Parkersburg this eaving. Staid all night at the solders rest. Thur 11. i took the train for Cumberland this morning. thair is 40 of us. Fri 12. we arived in Cumberland this morning and went in to the Convaleson camp. it is vary warm today. Sat 13. the wether is ofell hot. this is a misribell place to stay. i am vary lonsom today. Sun 14. it was vary hot in the four part of the day. this eaving we had a ofell storm. Mon 15. vary warm today. Tues 16. it raind vary hard this eaving. Wed 17. it raind today.

[61] Cumberland, Maryland
August the 17th 1864

Dear Sister,

it is with plazer that i take mi pen in hand this eaving to let you no that i am well at presant and i hope these fue lins will find you all the same. Well, i thout i wood of got to mi Co. but i mist it. i mite as well of staid at the hospital. i dont no when i well git to the

Co. Thair is about one thousand hear in the Convaleson camp. Harvey is hear. we have had som vary hard rains this week. well, i have not hurd from Alonzo, i beleve, since i wrote to you before. i think thay have gon up the valley again. well, i recon Isaac is at home. i hope so. tell him to take a good stay for it is no use to com hear. tell him he had better com to Roseberry Rock[32] and take the cars thair when he starts to com out. i think that wood be the safeist. Well i have 37 days to surve in the servis yet, then i will be at home. well thair is no news hear so i will close for the presant hopin to hear from you all soon. mi love to you all. good by

Joshua Winters

Drect your letters this way
Mr. Joshua Winters
Co. G. First Va Infantry
Convaleson Camp
Cumberland, MD

DIARY. Thur Aug 18. Cloudy and sum rain. Sun 21. it is vary warm and sultry today. it raind vary hard today. Tues 23. Clear and plesant today. Wed 24. Clear and warm today. we had a speach in camp tonight. Thur 25. it raind today. i started home today on the frait train. Fri 26. we arived at Cameron 11 this morning and walked home from thair.[33] got home at night. Sat 27. i rode out to Sand Hill today. Sun 28. i was at Church today. Mon 29. i went to Wheeling today. Tues 30. i was at home today. Wed 31. i was on the uther side of Haneytown at a diner and a speakin today. plesant day. Thurs, Sept 8 1864. i left Sand Hill this morning for Cameron. got thair at 9 oclock. staid all night. it raind vary hard. Fri 9. i took the cars this morning for Cumberland. got thair late in the eaving. Sat 10. it raind all day. i staid at the straglers camp.

---

[32] Now called Rosby's Rock, this landmark is a giant sandstone that is said to mark the location where the last spike was driven in the B. & O. Railroad when crews moving east met crews working from the west. *History of Marshall County WV, 1984,24.*

[33] It is at least fifteen miles from Cameron to the Winters farm.

[62] Cumberland Maryland
September the 10th [1864]

Dear Sister,

it is with plazer that i send you these fue lins to let you no that we got back hear safe. We got hear last night. we staid all night at Fries.[34] Isaac is not hear. thay left last week. we will start to our regement in the morning. i will rite as soon as i get thair. Fries is all well. no more at presant. From

to Kezia J. Winters Joshua Winters

[63] [From Isaac to sister Mary, after Isaac left the hospital in Parkersburg and returned to his unit.]

Camp at Summers Point
Jefferson County
September the 11, 1864

Dear sister,

it is with plesure that i seat My self to let you no that We are well at present and i hope that these few lines may find you injoying the same Blessin.

Well i have got to the Compney once more and i am glad of it. Thare has been 3 of the boys kill and 8 of them wouned since thay came to the valley but the Sand Hill boys is all safe yet but John Chedester.[35] He was shot in the leg last Sateday. Thare has been sum hard fighting dun here and sum hard fighting to do yet.

Dan Workman[36] came to the Compney the same day that I did. He was at Cherry Run. He is well.

Lol says he will not rite enney more till he gits a letter. I got a letter from Hannah[37] yesterday. Well all news is scarce. i will close

---

[34] Joshua's aunt, Rebecca Jane (Winters) Fry, husband John and children moved to the Cameron area before 1860.

[35] John Chidester was wounded at Berryville on Sept. 3, 1864. See note in Oct 19 letter.

[36] Daniel Workman was from Marshall County, and lived as a boy with a Conkell family next door to the Joshua Blake family. Census 1850. He enlisted in the Co. I of the Fifteenth at the same time that Isaac did and served the entire term.

[37] Hannah (Heatherington) Winters was Isaac's wife. They had a small son, Richard Isaac Winters. A family tale says Isaac carried one of Richard's booties in his breast uniform pocket during the war as a good luck charm .

by askin you to rite as soon as you git this.

So good by,
I. D. Winters to
Mary Winters

I still remain your brother till deth.

The First Va has to stay 2 mounth after thare time is out.

DIARY. Sun Sept. 11. it raind today. we left Cumberland on the cars this morning. got off at Hancock, crost the river thair. marched to Flintstone, campt all night. Mon 12. on our march this morning. went 21 mils. campt at Hagerstown, Md. Tues 13. nice day. on our march this morning earley. got to Sharpsburg at noon, 13 mils. campt in the church. Wed 14. it raind vary hard today. we got to Harpers Ferry, 10 mils. staid all night thair. Fri 16. we got to our regment 12 tonight. marched from Harpers Ferry today. Sun 18. plesant day. we fell in for a march today. the order countermanded. Mon 19. pleasant day. cananadin commenced at day light. all of the armey moved toards Winchester. muskitry vary heavey. our begaid was in it.[38] we garded the train and hospital. Co. G on pickit. Tues 20. the armey moved fourard earley this morning, drivin the rebs. we laid in camp all day at the hospital. the cavery maid thair apearance. Wed 21. plesant day. we laid at Opekin creek today. thay moved the wounded to Winchester. the armey moved to Strawsburg. sum fitin today. Thur 22. we moved earley this morning to Winchester, took the train out to Fisher's Hill. the fite commenced today vary hard. whipt them off the Fisher's Hill, capterd prisners. drove them in every drection. our loss slight.[39] Fri 23. the armey moved fourard this morning to Wookstock. campt thair. our Co. on pickit. sum cananadin this eaving. the eneme scatterd in every drection. cavery fite, drove rebs again. mi time is out today.[40] Sat Sept 24. we

---

[38] This was the Third Battle of Winchester, or Opequon Creek. Losses on both sides were heavy. The Federals were considered victors. Long, 571, Sept 19.

[39] The Battle of Fisher's Hill was considered a Union victory. The whole Union Army suffered 528 casualties while Confederate Gen. Early reported 1235. Long, 573, Sept 22.

[40] Joshua had enlisted for three years on 23 Sept 1861. According to his brothers Sept 11 letter the regiment had to remain in service two months longer.

moved this morning to New Market. cananadin today. the rebs is scatterd all over the valley. our min in good hart, fast movin.[41] Sun 25. today we moved to Harisinburg. all quiet today. the min vary tiard. Mon 26. laid in camp at Harisinburg today. Wed 28. we had orders to move this morning at 5 oclock. the order was countermanded. it raind today. Thurs 29. the 6 and 19 armey Coar left hear this morning, moved up the valley. we had Co. drill today.

Sun Oct 2. thair was a fite at Mount Croford today. the rebs repulst.[42] Thur 6. the armey fell back from Harisinbrug to Rudes Hill, 24 mils. all vary tiard. Sat 8. took up our lins of march this morning. campt in the vircinity of Fishers Hill. our begaid campt close to Strawsburg with the cavery. Sun 9. aleven peces of cannon, 25 wagons and sum prisners was fetched back today. Mon 10. we started for Martainsburg with the train today. Fri 14. our regement went on pickit tonight at Martainsburg.

[64]

U. S. Christian Commission

sends this as the Soldier's messenger to his Home. Let it hasten to those who wait for tidings.

"Behold! now is the accepted time; behold, now is the day of salvation."

CENTRAL OFFICE: 11 Bank Street, Philadelphia.

BRANCH OFFICE: 10th and H Streets, Washington.

October the 14th 1864
Martainsburg, West Va.

Dear Sister,

it is with plazer that i take mi pen in hand to let you no that i am in good helth and i hope these fue lins will find you all the same. Isaac and Lonzo is both well. thay ar close to Cedar Crick. our begaid came back with a train. we expect to go up tomorrow again.

---

[41] Long, 574, Sept 24: "In the Shenadoah Valley fighting occurred at Mt. Jackson, Luray, New Market, Forest Hill. Mainly, however, the defeated forces of Early - badly needing reorganization, rest and reinforcements - were retiring further."

[42] Long, 578, Oct 2: ".. skirmishing erupted at Mount Crawford and Bridgewater Va."

i expect to git home before the election. the reasin the boys hasant written ofner thay have no paper with them. i have writtin sum 4 or 5 since i came out and i have never got one yet. it has bin rite cold this week hear. thair is not mutch a goin on in the valley now. Well i will close, hopin to hear from you soon.

mi love to you all
Joshua Winters
to Anne M. Winters good by

DIARY. Sat October 15 1864. we left Martainsburg this eaving at 4 oclock with the train. com to Bunker Hill and campt 10 at night. it raind sum. Sun 16. we started earley this morning, got to Winchester at 12 oclock. campt thair. Mon 17. laid in camp all day. Tues 18. the battell of Cedar Crick fot on the 19. Col Thobern kild. the 1 devesion drove in confision from the uthworks.[43] we drove them in the eaving from Fishers Hill. Wed 19. we started from Winchester this morning to take the train to Cedar Crick. met the straglers a cumin in. we stopt them. the rebs drove our min in the forenoon from Cedar Crick. we drove them back, capterd artillry. our begaid laid in batell line at Winchester.[44]

[65] from Anna Maria Winters

Sand Hill
Marshall Co. West Va.
October 19, 1864

Dear Brother,

i once more take up my pen to inform you that we are all well and do hope you are the same. i have not got a letter for so long i thought i would write one by the way of introduction. i received one from Lol last night. he said you was well the last time he saw you and he said Isaac and him was both well at the time he had rote. Well Josse, there is no good news of importance to rite. Pap and Gabriel is working at the Buck Wheat. they said they would finish

---

[43] The First Division [Federal] was driven in confusion from the earthworks in the early morning. One of Joshua's favorite Colonels, Joseph Thoburn, was killed. The Federals drove them in the evening from Fisher's Hill.

[44] Long, Oct 19: Battle of Cedar Creek or Belle Grove, Va, described in detail on page 585, was a back-and-forth battle. "The Confederates were badly beaten but they made a gallant showing."

this evening. it lookes very much like rain this evening but i am in great hopes it wont rain for Pap and Mother and Ally is going to Wheeling in the morning.

Well Aunt Kizzia[45] has been up on a visit. she was in great hopes she would get to see you. Uncle Sam Reed[46] has been up on a visit and gone home agin. i got a letter from Lizzie[47] a Sundy. they are all well. She says that Uncle Will Davis[48] is drafted. Well i suppose you heard that John Chedister[49] is Dead. the word came last week and also Joseph Douglas[50] is Dead. the word came a Sunday and i heard yesterday that Alexander Shilling[51] is Dead. i dont no fer certain wither it is so or not. Well there is a great deal of sickness about here now. Will Dague has the fever but was better the last we heard from him. Robert Taylor[52] has the typhoid fever very bad. there is to be a union speaking at Sand Hill a Friday next. there is to be a high time at Haney Town next Tuesday and Wensday. there is to be a dinner each day, a half a dollar a piece and the money to go to the soilders if they get it. there is to be about twenty preachers there. Well i must write to Lol and to Lib this evening. when you write tell us when you think you will get home again. i heard not till the fifteenth, so Cornel Weddel rote to

---

[45] Keziah (Davis) Keller, sister of Joshua's mother. She lived in Peoria County IL, apparently "home" for a visit.

[46] Sam's wife was Joshua's Aunt Jane (Davis) Reed, sister of his mother. Aunt Jane died in Peoria County IL in 1856. Sam still lived in Peoria County.

[47] Joshua's sister, Elizabeth Rogers. She was living in Peroia County at this time.

[48] Uncle Will was the husband of Joshua's Aunt Elizabeth (Davis) Davis, his mother's sister. They went to Peoria County in 1856.

[49] John was in Isaac Winters Company. He was wounded in the leg at Berryville on Sept 3, 1864, discharged on Sept 13, and died of his wounds. Powell, 239. He had a wife Rachel and at least three children. Census. He died at Sandy Hook MD of wounds received at Berryville. Adj. Gen. Rept. 1865, 224.

[50] The only Joseph Douglas in Marshall County in 1860 lived near the Winters' on Sand Hill and was a son in the large family of William and Mary Douglas, but was age 10 at that time. Joseph was not in the area in 1870. Census.

[51] This may have been premature unless there were two Alexander Shillings'. The Alexander, age 23, son of Murray and Hannah, in the 1860 census, enlisted Aug 16 1862 in Co. A of the Twelfth West Virginia was discharged June 16, 1865. Powell, 226. He was living with wife Jane and three children in Sand Hill District in 1870. Census.

[52] Robert Taylor, age 25, wife Susan and son, Fair View P. O. in 1860. Susan with children in 1870. Maybe Robert died of typhoid.

his wife i heard.

Well there is great talk about the election here now. there is a great many about here that goes in for McClelan but i think Abe will carry the day.[53] i hope so at least. Some thinks that if Abe gets it again the war wont be over for four years longer, but i am in hopes that it will end this fall at the furtherest. Well i must rite to Lib yet and it is pretty near supper time now so i must quit riting for this time. please to answer soon and i will rite again. i am in hopes you will get home next month any how. Please to excuse this scribbling and rite soon. No more at this time. Mother and Pap and all the rest send their love to you. My love to you and all enquiring soilders. From your sister

Anna M. Winters

To Joshua Winters. Write soon.

DIARY. Thur Oct 20 1864. we left Winchester 1 oclock this morning. took the train to Cedar Creek then campt thair. prisners still acomin in. movin all the wounded back. hard battell. ofell sites on the field.[54] Fri 21. it rained tonight. we moved back this morning to Newton to gard the hospittell. i am on gard tonight. the prisners sent back today. Sat 22. vary winday today. Tues 25. i am on gard tonight at head qurters.

[66] Camp at Newtown betwean
Winchester and Cedar Crick
8 miles from the main army
it is in Camp at Cedar Crick

October the 26th 1864

Dear Sister,

it is with plazer that i take mi pennsyl in hand this eaving to let you no that i am well and i hope these fue lins will find you all in good helth. i saw Isaac and Alonzo just 5 days ago. thay was both well and all the rest of the boys well. we have had a nuther hard battel in the valley and a Gloryous Victory it was. Thay supprised

---

[53] Abraham Lincoln, running for re-election, was opposed by the Democratic candidate General George B. McClellan. Of course, Abe carried the day.

[54] The aftermath of the Battle of Cedar Creek.

Crucks[55] Command and whipt them pretty bad in the morning but it turned in the eaving and we gave them an an ofell whippin. all the Sand Hill boys in the 15th is safe. nun hurt that you no. we wasant in it. our bregade was at Winchester. we had just started to take the train up when we hurd the fitin and the straglers was a cumin and wagens a cumin in every derection. we stopt them then. we didant go up till the next day. then we took the train up to the army, staid thair one day, then com back hear to this littel town to gard the hospittal. our bregaid has bin vary luckey. we havant bin in enne fite since i com to the regement but we have had our shear of goin up and down the valley with the train. the boys in the 15th lost every thing thay had but thay was luckey in gittin out safe but it was a vary hard fite. the loss was heavey on both sides.

we all miss our Colonell[56] vary mutch. we ar a gittin a long vary well hear but we have a good deal of duty to do. it is rite cool hear at night. Jake is on safe gard three miles from Camp at a house. thay keep him. he gits a long vary well. well we will be home inside of 18 days if nuthing happens. i received your letter last night, the first one since i com out. i was vary glad to hear from you once more. well it is time i was a gittin supper for mi self. the boys is on pickit. i am a lone in the tent to night. i expect it to be cold. mi love to you all. no more from your brother,

Joshua Winters.

Anne M. Winters. Good by.

you must excuse this bad writing and spelling[57] for i cant write with a led pensell. this paper got wet in my polk.[58] dont make fun of it. i have no more.

DIARY. Thur Oct 27. i am on pickit tonight. it raind studdy all night. Fri 28. it is vary winday today. the forge train was attacked today. the 4 and 12 Va regement went out on Dubell Crick. our regement fell in and stacked arms. Sun 30. we left Newtown this

[55] George Crook, commanding one of Sheridan's corps, led the Battle of Fisher's Hill on Sept 22. Long, 573.

[56] Colonel Joseph Thoburn who was killed at the Battle of Cedar Creek on Oct 19.

[57] The reader knows by now that more than a "led pensel" interferes with Joshua's spelling!

[58] A poke is a West Virginia colloquism meaning sack or bag.

morning at 8. past through Winchester, got to Martainsburgh at 9 oclock at night. all vary tiard. we marched the distance of 31 mils. Mon 31. we laid at Martainsburgh till 4 in the eaving, then we took the cars fur Cumberland. it was rite cold today.

Tuesday November 1 1864. we arived at Cumberland this morning and went in to camp. Wed 2. i washed mi clothes today. it raind tonight. Thur 3. today it is dark, cold, and drislin rain. Sat. 12. we left Cumberland this eaving for Wheeling. the vetterns staid. we got to Peadmont at 10 oclock. staid all night in the cars, vary cold. Sun 13. vary cold. the cars moved off this morning. we got to Grafton at dark. all putnear froze. Mon 14. we arived in Wheeling this morning, all vary tiard of our ride. we came putnear freezin. all the boys started for home. Sat Nov. 26. i was discharged from the United States Survis today at Wheeling. Mon 28. i was paid today and got mi papers. I AM FREE ONCE MORE.

In the back of the diary, in his best penmanship, it says:

DECEMBER.—BILLS PAYABLE.

Date.	NAME.	Dollars.	Ce
	Joshua Winters Co G		
	9th West VA		
	Parkersburg West VA		
	July the 11th 1864		

Oh love is to the human heart
What sunshine is to flowers.
And friendship is the fairest thing
In this cold world of ours.

[End of Joshua's writings.]

JOSHUA WINTERS discharge reads:

Know ye, that Joshua Winters a private of Captain Oscar F. Melvins Company G, First Regiment of the West Virginia Infantry Volunteers who was enrolled on the twenty third of September one thousand eight hundred and sixty one to serve three years or during the war, is hereby DISCHARGED from the service of the United States, this twenty sixth day of November, 1864, at Wheeling W Va by reason of expiration of term of service. (No objection of his re-enlistment is known to exist.)

Said Joshua Winters was born in Marshall County in the State of West Virginia, is nineteen years of age, Six feet 0 inches high, fair complexion, grey eyes, dark hair, and by occupation, when enrolled, a farmer.

Given at Wheeling, W. Va. this twenty sixth day of November 1864.

well anne our tent smokes to bad to
write and i cant think of enne thing to write
father tell nance that i will write to hur
this week tell me if alle has got thair
present from wheeling yet or not well
you will haf to excuse me for not writing
more this time i will write more the next
so giv mi love to all of you nomore
at present but remain your brother
Joshua Winters

Anne M Winters

write soon good by
write soon as you can

this is the way to direct your letters

Mr Joshua Winters
Romney hampshire Co. va
in Cair of Capton Melvin
Co G First va reg infantry

and for gracious sake dont put haste
on the back of the letter nor soilder nor
nuthing els now dont for git

Appendix A

Annual Report of the Adjutant General of the State of West Virginia
December 1864

Record of Captain Oscar F. Melvin's Company "G," First West Virginia Volunteer Infantry, showing the changes in said Company from the date of organization to the date of muster-out on the 26th day of November, 1864, by Lieut. Henry C. Peck, 14th U.S. Infantry. Compiled from muster-out rolls.

Name	Rank	Age	When mustered into service	Remarks
Melvin, Oscar F.	Capt	24	Oct.30,1861	
Lloyd. Thomas	1st Lt	33	Oct.30,1861	
Hall, Chester B.	2d Lt	22	Oct.30,1861	Trans. to Co.D
Robb, Williams J.	2d Lt	40	Oct.30,1861	Trans. to Co.A
Adams, Joseph O.	2d Lt	25	Oct.30,1861	Prom. from Sgt
Blankinship, Jno. Jr.	Serg't	23	Oct.30,1861	Wounded at Piedmont Va. June 5, 1864
Wark, David	Serg't	32	Oct.30,1861	
Stroble, Robert W.	Corp'l	25	Oct.30,1861	
Corbley, Eli C.	Corp'l	21	Oct.30,1861	
Goudy, William	Corp'l	21	Oct.30,1861	
Brashear, Brise	Priv	22	Oct.30,1861	
Coates, Jacob	Priv	30	Oct.30,1861	
Corbley, Andrew	Priv	20	Oct.30,1861	
Crawford, Oscar F.	Priv	21	Oct.30,1861	
Hall, William	Priv	21	Oct.30,1861	
Howard, William	Priv	31	Oct.30,1861	
Moren, Robert	Priv	28	Oct.30,1861	
Parrish, James S.	Priv	18	Oct.30,1861	
Riddle, Clark	Priv	24	Oct.30,1861	
Soles, Jacob	Priv	19	Oct.30,1861	
Thompson, Oliver B.	Priv	18	Oct.30,1861	
Winters, Joshua	Priv	19	Oct.30,1861	

Name	Rank	Age	When mustered into service	Remarks
Prisoners of War				
Shrimplin, William G.	Priv	30	Oct.30,1861	Captured at New Market, Va. 5/15/64
Recuits				
Barcus, David	Priv	18	Mar.23,1862	Not mustered out.
Crawford, George G.	Priv	23	Aug.4, 1862	" " "
Cunningham, S. W.	Priv	19	Feb.23,1864	" " "
Cook, James	Priv	22	Feb.25,1864	" " "
Cannan, John C.	Priv	28	Mar.22,1864	" " "
Gonter, Hoseph M.	Priv	30	Feb.23,1864	" " "
Nichols, James C.	Priv	24	Mar.22,1864	" " "
Shriner, William	Priv	24	Aug.11,1862	" " "
Smith, Andrew G.	Priv	20	Mar.24,1864	" " "
Wayble, Cyrus H.	Priv	25	Mar.7, 1864	" " "
Veterans,				
Melvin, William H.	1st Sgt	21	Oct.30,1861	Re-enlis,d Feb 8 1864
Good, Thomas C.	Serg't	33	Oct.30,1861	Re-enls'd Feb 22 1864
Edie, George W.	Corp'l	18	Oct.30,1861	Re-enls'd Feb 22 1864
Montgomery, George	Corp'l	20	Oct.30,1861	Re-enlis'd Feb 8 1864
Brownlee, William	Corp'l	27	Oct.30,1861	Re-enlis'd Feb 8 1864
Cord, William	Corp'l	18	Oct.30,1861	Re-enls'd Jan 26 1864
Frazier, George A	Corp'l	20	Oct.30,1861	Re-enlis'd Feb 8 1864
Adams, John	Priv.	18	Oct.30,1861	Re-enlis'd Feb 8 1864
Armstrong, C. B.	Priv.	21	Oct.30,1861	Re-enls'd Jan 26 1864
Barnes, Shepley	Priv.	22	Oct.30,1861	Re-enlis'd Feb 8 1864
Connell, John R.	Priv.	21	Oct.30,1861	Re-enlis'd Feb 8 1864
Curfman, Joshua	Priv.	18	Oct.30,1861	Re-enlis'd Feb 8 1864
Edie, John N.	Priv.	19	Oct.30,1861	Re-enlis'd Feb 8 1864
Kelley, John	Priv.	40	Oct.30,1861	Re-enlis'd Feb 8 1864
Kerr, Daniel L.	Priv.	21	Oct.30,1861	Re-enlis'd Feb 8 1864
McCausland, Robert	Priv.	28	Oct.30,1861	Re-enlis'd Feb 8 1864
McAdams, John T.	Priv.	25	Oct.30,1861	Re-enls'd Feb 22 1864
Nichols, Edward	Priv.	28	Oct.30,1861	Re-enls'd Jan 26 1864
Pugh, John C.	Priv	23	Oct.30,1861	Re-enlis'd Feb 8 1864

Name	Rank	Age	When mustered into service	Remarks
Plattenburg, Jno. W	Priv	21	Oct.30,1861	Re-enlis'd Feb 8 1864
Robinett, James	Priv	27	Oct.30,1861	Re-enls'd Jan 26 1864
Rose, James T.	Priv.	21	Oct.30,1861	Re-enlis'd Feb 8 1864
Shriner, Peter	Priv.	36	Oct.30,1861	Re-enlis'd Feb 8 1864
Shearer, Andrew J.	Priv.	23	Oct.30,1861	Re-enlis'd Feb 8 1864
Torreyson, F. M.	Priv.	28	Oct.30,1861	Re-enlis'd Feb 8 1864
Wark, Charles	Priv.	32	Oct.30,1861	Re-enls'd Feb 22 1864
Williams, Valentine	Priv.	24	Oct.30,1861	Re-enlis'd Feb 8 1864
Zimmerman, Frank	Priv.	18	Oct.30,1861	Re-enlis'd Feb 8 1864
Bonsall, Albert E.	Priv.	18	Oct.30,1861	Re-enl'd Aug 30 1864
Discharged				
Clochan, William	Serg't	23	Oct.30,1861	March 1 1862 promotion in Co. K
Morrow, James E.	Serg't	24	Oct.30,1861	March 1 1862 promotion in Co. E
Plattenburg, Jno. W	Serg't	31	Oct.30,1861	March 24 promotion in Co. K
Haney, James M.	Corp'l	21	Oct.30,1861	Jun 29 1862 disability
Leazear, James	Corp'l	24	Oct.30,1861	Sep 29 1862 disability
Nichols, Robert Jr.	Mus'n	31	Oct.30,1861	Jun 29 1862 disability
Bonsall, John A	Priv.	38	Oct.30,1861	Sept 1862 disability
Calendine, Samuel	Priv.	41	Oct.30,1861	Jan 15 1862 disability
Camhouse, John	Priv.	34	Oct.30,1861	March 1863 disability
Cruson, John	Priv.	21	Oct.30,1861	Nov 14 1862
Dowler, John F.	Priv.	26	Oct.30,1861	Nov 10 1862
Glass, John	Priv.	24	Aug.5,1862	Nov 14 1862
Jones, Isaac	Priv.	22	Mar.3,1862	Aug 2 1862 disability
Johnson, Isaac	Priv.	24	Mar.3,1862	Nov 11 1862 disability
Letzikus, Josehp	Priv.	22	Jan.28,1862	Dec 14 1862 disability
Langworth, Horace	Priv.	29	Oct.30,1861	Mar 25 1863 disability
Lowry, Calvin	Priv.	29	Oct.30,1861	Feb 2 1863 disability
Leazear, George W.	Priv.	19	Oct.30,1861	Mar 11 1863 disability
Marshall, Wm. A.	Priv.	23	Jan.28,1862	Nov 11 1862 disability
McCann, Samuel	Priv.	24	Oct.30,1861	Nov. 17 1862
McConkey, Joseph	Priv.	44	Oct.30,1861	Jun 29 1862 disability

Name	Rank	Age	When mustered into service	Remarks
McCoy, Samuel G.	Priv.	20	Oct.30,1861	Nov 14 1862
McSwords, James	Priv.	27	Oct.30,1861	Oct 31 1862 disability
Nangle, Samuel G.	Priv.	21	Jan.28,1862	Jun 29 1862 disability
Parsons, Benj. L.	Priv.	24	Oct.30,1861	Nov 19 1862 disability
Springer, William	Priv.	22	Oct.30,1861	Jan 26 1863
Whitham, Philip	Priv.	38	Oct.30,1861	Sept 1862 disability
Woodward, Jos. H.	Priv.	18	Oct.30,1861	Jan 5 1863 disability
Transferred				
Bonsall, Wm. G.	Serg't	20	Oct.30,1861	Pro.Q.M.Sgt.Mar 1863
Johnson, Henry J.	Corp'l	19	Oct.30,1861	Pro. Sgt.Maj.Jan 1863
Ball, Richard	Priv.	19	Oct.30,1861	Transferred to V.R.C.
Dillon, Thomas J.	Priv.	19	Oct.30,1861	Transferred to V.R.C.
Wilson, James	Priv.	41	Oct.30,1861	Prom. Nov 9 1861
				died
McHenry, Benjamin	Priv.	23	Oct.30,1861	Measles, Feb 2 1862
Noon, Thomas	Priv.	19	Oct.30,1861	Disease, May 11 1862
Shriner, John	Priv.	19	Oct.30,1861	Wounds,June 16 1864
Gosnell, John	Priv.	18	Oct.30,1861	Killed in action July 24 1864
Deserted				
Cochran, Thomas J.	Priv.	18	Oct.30,1861	Dec 2, 1862

Aggregate.............. 101 men.

Appendix B

A Brief Genealogy of Joshua Winters' Family
Brothers, Sisters, Aunts, Uncles and Cousins

Joshua made frequent references in his letters to various relatives. This genealogy is presented to help the interested reader understand the nature of the relationships.

Joshua's parents were John and Eliza (Davis) Winters, both of whom had been born in the area that is now Sand Hill District, Marshall County, WV. They lived there all their lives. Their children, Joshua's siblings, were:

1. Kezia Jane Winters, born 25 Oct 1831, died 1891, never married.
2. Mary Ellen Winters, born 4 Aug 1834, died 1870, never married.
3. Isaac Davis Winters, born 8 Oct 1835, married Hannah Heatherington and raised nine children. He died in 1917. Isaac was the great-grandfather of this editor.
4. Elizabeth Winters, born 26 Dec 1838, married James Rogers and had three sons. She died in 1869.
5. Alonzo Winters, born May 1841, married Margaret McCracken and had three children. He died in 1923.
6. Joshua Winters, born 8 Jan 1843, married Beulah Jane Blake and raised two children. He died in 1900.
7. Anne Maria Winters, born in 1845 and never married. She died in 1923.
8. Easter Rebecca Winters, born 12 Dec 1846, married William Dague and had seven children. She died in 1923.
9. Susan Nancy Winters, born March 1848, married John Hudson Davis and raised three sons. She died in 1916.
10. Alice Eliza Winters, born 2 Dec 1849, married James A. Dague and raised six children. She died in 1896.

All the children were born, lived their lives, and raised their families in Sand Hill District, Marshall County, now WV. (Elizabeth did reside for a few years in Peoria County, IL.) All but Easter are buried in the Sand Hill Cemetery. Easter is buried at Mount View Cemetery in Dallas.

Joshua had no living grandparents at the time of his Civil War service, but both sets of grandparents had lived in Sand Hill District since about 1804, and raised large families. Many of their children and grandchildren lived in the area and were mentioned in Joshua's or Annie's letters.

Daniel Winters was born in Ireland and came to (W.) Va. through Pennsylvania, where his wife was born. The children of Daniel and Mary (Blake) Winters, thus Joshua's paternal aunts and uncles, were:

1. James Winters, born 1803 in PA, married Rebecca Cunningham. Their sons were John Wesley Winters, Daniel Winters, James Franklin Winters, Thomas Jefferson Winters, and William Harvey Winters. Several of these boys went by their middle names. James died in 1872.
2. John Winters, was born 17 Oct 1806 in the present Sand Hill District, married Eliza Davis. Their family is detailed above.
3. Easter Winters, born 1808, married John Wherry.
4. Elizabeth Winters, born 1810, called Betsey, married John Creighton.
5. Samuel Winters, born 1812, moved to Ohio in 1837.
6. Margaret Winters, born 1814, apparently died young.
7. Mary Winters, born 15 June 1817, married Robert Daugherty. She is the "Aunt Polly" mentioned. They lived on a farm adjoining the Winters family. Among their children were James W. Daugherty, John W. Daugherty, Robert H. Daugherty, Daniel W. Daugherty, Nancy E. Daugherty, and others.
8. Nancy Winters, born in 1820, was the second wife of Hanson Davis. Hanson's children were from his first marriage. See below.
9. Daniel Winters, born 17 March 1821, married Margaret Hartley. They raised two daughters.
10. Rebecca Jane Winters, born 1824-5, married John Frey. They lived near Cameron during the Civil War and Joshua spent a night at their house on his way back to camp.

Joshua's maternal grandparents were Isaac and Keziah (Askew) Davis. They were born in Maryland where their ancestors had lived for several generations. Their children, also Joshua's aunts and uncles, were:

1. Albert Davis, born 20 Jan 1805, married Mary Rodefer, another descendant of early pioneers, and they lived on Big Wheeling Creek. Their children, Silas Rodefer Davis and Eliza Jane Mooney lived in Sand Hill District. The others had moved to Peoria County IL. Silas was EDS great-grandfather.
2. Eliza Davis, born 22 Sept 1806, married John Winters. Their family is detailed above.
3. Hanson Davis, born 14 Dec 1808, married (1st) Mary Cunningham, (2nd) Nancy Winters. Some of his children were Albert G. Davis, John Hudson Davis, who was in the Fifteenth Regiment, Sarah Jane Turner, whose husband Samuel was in the Fifteenth Regiment, and Annie Rebecca Rogers, the second wife of James Rogers, married after her cousin Elizabeth (Winters) Rogers died in childbirth. Hanson had two daughters, Kezia and Mary, who married Daugherty boys. Mary's spouse was John W. Duagherty, a first cousin of Joshua. The other Daugherty, Robert, was John's cousin. Most of these families lived in the Sand Hill area during the Civil War.
4. Ann Maria Davis, born 1811, married John Bonnett. They lived near Marysville OH and had three sons in the Union Army.
5. Mary Davis, born 5 May 1814. She was single and died in 1833.
6. Elizabeth Davis, born 1816, married William C. Davis. They lived in Peoria County IL. Annie mentioned in a letter that "Uncle Will Davis" had been drafted. The editor knows nothing of his Civil War Service.
7. Joshua Davis, born 1815/1820, died 1843/1850.
8. Kezia Davis, born 1822, married John R. Keller. They lived in Peoria County IL.
9. Jane Davis, born 16 June 1825, married Samuel M. Reed. They lived in Peoria County IL. Jane died in 1856, and Samuel remarried.
10. Susan Davis, born 19 July 1828, married John Supler. She died in childbirth in Louisville KY in 1852 and John remarried.

References Cited

Adjutant General. *Annual Report of the Adjutant General of the State of West Virginia for the year ending December 31, 1864.* John Frew, Printer, Wheeling, WV, 1865.

Adjutant General. *Annual Report of the Adjutant General of the State of West Virginia for the year ending December 31, 1863.* John Frew, Printer, Wheeling, WV, 1864.

Briggs, Ethel and Ada Finnicum, compilers, from U. S. Dept. of the Census microfilm. *1850 Census of Marshall County W. Va.* Tri-County Researchers, New Martinsville, WV, 1981.

Briggs, Ethel and Ada Finnicum, compilers, from U. S. Dept. of the Census microfilm. *1860 Federal Census of Marshall County (West) Virginia.* Tri-County Researchers, New Martinsville, WV, 1983.

Briggs, Ethel and Ada Finnicum, compilers, from U. S. Dept. of the Census microfilm. *1870 Federal Census of Marshall County, West Virginia.* Tri-County Researchers, New Martinsville, WV, 1985.

Cohen, Stan B. *A Pictorial Guide to West Virginia's Civil War Sites and Related Information.* Pictorial Histories Publishing Company, Charleston, WV, 1990.

Long, E. B. with Barbara Long. *The Civil War Day by Day: An Almanac; 1861-1865.* Doubleday & Company, Garden City, NY, 1971.

McConnell, Mildred M. et al. *Wheeling's First 250 Years.* National Bank of West Virginia, Wheeling WV, 1942.

Powell, Scott. *History of Marshall County, West Virginia.* Moundsville, WV, 1925.

Strother, David H., edited by Cecil D. Eby. *The Diaries of David Hunter Strother; A Virginia Yankee in the Civil War.* The University of North Carolina Press, Chapel Hill, NC, 1961.

U. S. Army. *Military Service Records of Volunteer Soldiers.* National Archives and Records Service. Civil War Military and Pension Records.

U. S. Bureau of the Census. *1890 Special Schedule-Surviving Soldiers, Sailors, and Marines, and Widows, etc. Marshall County, WV.* Microfilm.

Index

Notes

Notes